C000142650

The Gazette

AT THE HEART OF HEMEL HEMPSTEAD, BERKHAMSTED, TRING AND THE LANGLEYS — EST 1859

HEMEL HEMPSTEAD
BERKHAMSTED & TRING
A Century of Change

The Gazette

AT THE HEART OF HEMEL HEMPSTEAD, BERKHAMSTED, TRING AND THE LANGLEYS — EST 1859

HEMEL HEMPSTEAD
BERKHAMSTED & TRING
A Century of Change

breedon **books**
PUBLISHING

First published in Great Britain in 2002 by
The Breedon Books Publishing Company Limited
Breedon House, 3 The Parker Centre,
Derby, DE21 4SZ.

© HEMEL HEMPSTEAD GAZETTE 2002

All Rights Reserved. No part of this publication may be reproduced, stored in
a retrieval system, or transmitted in any form, or by any means, electronic,
mechanical, photocopying, recording or otherwise without the prior
permission in writing of the copyright holders, nor be otherwise circulated in
any form or binding or cover other than in which it is published and without a
similar condition being imposed on the subsequent publisher.

ISBN 1 85983 328 4

Printed and bound by Butler & Tanner, Frome, Somerset, England.
Cover printing by Lawrence-Allen Colour Printers, Weston-super-Mare,
Somerset, England.

Contents

Acknowledgements

We are grateful to English Partnerships, the successor to the Hemel Hempstead Development Corporation and the Commission for the New Towns, for their permission to reproduce some of their pictures, to Dacorum Heritage Trust and its curator Matt Wheeler for his help over the years – and last, but definitely not least, a big thank you to all the readers who have helped build up this eclectic archive of photographs, most of which have appeared at one time or another in the *Gazette's* Heritage series.

Prologue

THE *Gazette's* archives, which range from Queen Victoria to highwayman James Snook, from typhoid epidemics to Dacorum's woewater, have been necessarily distilled to fit into the confines of these pages.

There have been high profile casualties and mysterious omissions along the way; and what remains is neither a systematic, comprehensive nor strictly chronological treatment of Dacorum's history during the 20th century.

It is, nevertheless, an accurate portfolio of the pooled recollections of our readers – readers who are, in a sense, co-authors of this book: for it is they who have built up the archives over the years, with their photos, their postcards and their memories.

If the book has a focus, it is the three decades between the mid-1940s and the early 1970s – the three decades that resculptured Hemel Hempstead from a semi-rural backwater into an ever-expanding New Town.

So, the populace's reluctant acceptance of Satellite Town No. 3 and its passage from Whitehall blueprint to bricks and mortar takes up much, but not all, of our time.

In addition, there are brief detours through turn-of-the-century Dacorum's cress beds, wharves and world famous mills; and under its war-darkened skies.

Captains of Industry

ALONGSIDE its reputation as the home of paper, Hemel Hempstead's other claim to fame, from early Victorian times to the 1950s, was watercress.

But the popularity of the crop waned dramatically during the latter part of the 20th century and what was once a thriving industry has now vanished.

Hemel Hempstead's springs and artesian wells, from which water came at a constant temperature of 52F, made this area ideal for watercress.

Apart from the cress beds around Bourne End, there were beds at Water End, in the centre of Hemel Hempstead (now the Water Gardens), Two Waters and Berkhamsted.

The coming of the railways meant the local cress industry really took off – it was, and is, a crop that needs to get to the market quickly.

In those days the tomato was practically unknown and the Dutch and Spanish salad-producing industries of today had not even been thought of.

'Winkles and Cress' was the cry of many a street trader in London and other major cities. Most of Hemel Hempstead's cress went north as London's supply came from areas south of the Thames.

As the cress was gathered it was packed in large withy baskets made of willow and known as flats. Each flat weighed around 200cwt – a good day's picking could weigh two tons. In later days the flats were replaced by chipped boxes and the watercress was bunched.

During World War Two, home produced watercress, which is rich in calcium and iron, was much in demand, but why did that demand just fade away through the 1950s and 60s?

A lot of the blame must go to the nationalisation of the railways. The porters were reluctant to lift and carry heavy boxes of watercress from cart to train and the railways stopped paying compensation to the cress growers if the cress failed to get to market on time. Then there was Dr Beeching axing railway lines.

It wasn't all down to the trains, of course. Cress was a crop that had to be looked after in the shops – kept at the back, ideally in water – and as larger shops and supermarkets developed many of the traditional greengrocers disappeared.

Then there was an outbreak of crook root, a disease very similar to club root in green vegetables, that attacked crops nationally in the 1950s. And, finally, people's tastes changed.

The straw plait industry

Thousands of people in Hertfordshire found employment in the straw plait industry, but Chinese imports eventually put paid to the trade and few people remember just how important it was.

Luton's link with the straw plait industry is well known, but Hemel Hempstead was Luton's main supplier. In fact, the Nicky Line railway was first built to help take the plait to Luton. Sadly, the line took 15 years to get off the ground and during this time Chinese imports all but destroyed the local plait industry.

Hemel Hempstead had its own plait market behind the High Street in an alley by the Bell. Business got so brisk that a bigger market opened to the rear and side of the Kings Arms. Special types of straw for plaiting were grown locally and it was a real cottage industry.

Father cut the straw and bleached it with sulphur. The women and children then made the plait. Plaiting was also often done by children in plaiting schools – a practice stamped out by the Education Act of 1870.

Ovaltine

Ovaltine is one of the best known brand names to come from the Dacorum area.

Along with the drink, still enjoyed around the world today, came the Ovaltineys – or the League of Ovaltineys to give them their full title.

Their meteoric rise to fame began on Radio Luxembourg. The seven golden rules for being an Ovaltiney started with a promise 'to do the things that my parents tell me to, I want them to be proud of me and everything I do.'

Rule six, of course, was 'every day to drink my delicious Ovaltine, to make me fit and happy, with a mind that's bright and keen.'

Wander, the makers of Ovaltine, arrived in the area in 1929 when they bought two farms – Parsonage Farm at Abbots Langley and Numbers Farm at Kings Langley. They became known as the Modern Dairy Farm and the Modern Poultry Farm and were part of the company's promotion strategy and modelled as replicas of the Farm created by Louis XIV for Marie Antoinette.

Rose's Lime Juice

Hemel Hempstead's industrial growth through the mills and businesses that sprung up alongside the Grand Union Canal – for example, John Dickinson, Ovaltine and the timber yards and flour mills at Tring – has been well chronicled.

One of the last businesses to come to the canal and the last to use the waterway in a big way as its major link with its suppliers was Rose's Lime Juice.

The Rose family were shipbuilders from Leith, near Edinburgh, who set up a branch of their business to provide ships with supplies – including lime juice.

Lime juice, of course, was a remedy against scurvy and the Merchant Shipping Act of 1867 made it compulsory for all ocean going ships to carry a lime juice ration.

Demand increased and Lauchlan Rose realised that, although the neat lime juice taken for medicinal purposes by sailors might not be everyone's cup of tea, a sweetened, bottled and attractively labelled lime juice could well become popular in Britain.

With that in mind, he introduced the first branded fruit juice drink – Rose's Lime Juice. In 1893 he bought estates in Dominica and planted lime trees to supply the demand for his new drink.

By 1924, lime juice had become so popular that the company established new lime plantations on the Gold Coast to supplement supplies. The company moved from Edinburgh to London and Liverpool, but during World War Two the London branch in Worship Street was badly damaged by bombing and the company came to St Albans.

From 1947, the unprocessed lime juice arrived by ship at London's docks and the casks were transported by barge down the canal to Boxmoor.

Here, the juice was stored in huge oak vats, each holding up to 12,000 gallons. After a time the clear green-gold juice was drawn off, filtered and sweetened with pure sugar, then bottled in St Albans.

An unrecognisable Marlowes in the pre-war years.

Traditional boat building once thrived in Dacorum's boatyards.

Marlowes has always been peppered with shops – but these small retailers were swept away by the new town revolution.

A bird's-eye view of the canal – one of the engines of the area's economic growth.

Dacorum's workers let off steam with a pleasure cruise on the canal.

Berkhamsted's stretch of the
Grand Union Canal supported a
plethora of towpath businesses.

An early flying machine passes
precariously above Boxmoor
Station in 1910.

The High Street at the turn of the century.

A huge crowd gathers for the proclamation of Edward VII at the bottom of the High Street.

Crowds mill around the old town's market to hear the proclamation of Edward VII.

Foster's sawmill on the banks of the canal.

A barge laden with goods glides past a canal bridge.

Berkhamsted's mills were a major source of the town's prosperity.

The old lime kilns in Bennetts End.

Hemel Hempstead's most important industry was papermaking; another was the cultivation of watercress as shown in these two pictures. At one time, there were cress beds in Bourne End, Water End and Two Waters. Gathering cress was heavy work. It was packed in large withy baskets known as 'flats'. Each flat weighed around 200cwt – and a good day's picking could weigh as much as two tons. No wonder Harry Austin, Fred Sharp and his son John look a little weary in our picture.

More early last century picking and sorting of watercress.

Wander, the makers of Ovaltine, moved into Langleys in a big way in 1929. The company snapped up two farms in the area – Parsonage Farm at Abbots Langley and Numbers Farm at Kings Langley. They were part of the company's promotion strategy and modelled as replicas of the farm created by Louis XIV for Marie Antoinette. Almost 50 years later, in 1975, the beginning of the end was signalled by demolition work on the famous Ovaltine chimney. The 185ft chimney was taken down brick by brick – 250,000 of them in all. The first brick was presented to Charlie Appleby who had helped build the landmark 50 years earlier. Somewhat perversely, the chimney cost £7,000 to build but £8,000 to dismantle.

More pictures of the Ovaltine farm and works.

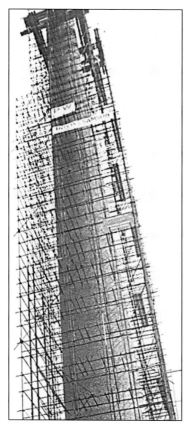

The famous Ovaltine chimney

A brick from the demolished chimney is presented to Charlie Appleby, one of the workers who helped in its original construction.

Berkhamsted's mantle factory employed hundreds of local people for around 80 years. The factory, in Lower Kings Road, was built in the 1890s and expanded in the 1920s, at which point the owners bought a sports ground at Cow Roast for their employees. It finally closed on Christmas Day, 1969. The company, which made ladies' clothing, was bought in 1919 by Corby, Palmer and Stewart amid considerable controversy – while residents campaigned for Berkhamsted to remain a residential town directly after World War One, the chamber of commerce wanted to entice new firms into the area. In the end, the mantle factory ended up employing some 800 workers. Unusually for a Victorian factory, the grand old building, which stood where Waitrose is today, was described as 'fitted throughout in a way that is not only the best for manufacturing but also that is most desirable for the health and happiness of the employees'.

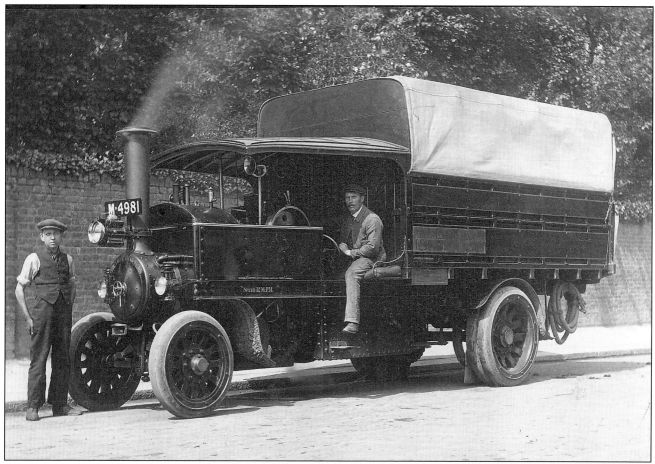

This steam-powered lorry transported Kent's brushes from Apsley to London. Kent's opened in 1901 in Apsley and is one of the few business that survived the entire century.

The straw plaiting school in Potten End employed many local children in the first half of the 19th century, but by the late 1890s, the cottage industry had been largely killed off by cheaper foreign imports.

Bennetts End Dairies, which once delivered the town's milk by horse and cart, was based behind the Princess Cinema near what is now Dacorum Civic Centre. The firm was bought by the Hammond family in 1921 and renamed Hygienic Dairies. Hygienic were the first dairy in Hertfordshire to introduce pasteurised milk. By the 1940s, the firm had a fleet of lorries. In 1951, Hygienic was bought out by Express Dairies.

Rose's Lime Juice was the last major business to come to the Grand Union Canal and the last to use the waterway as a major link to its suppliers. The company only came to Boxmoor Wharf in 1947, but its history stretches back to the mid-19th century. The piles of wooden barrels on the wharf were a familiar sight for more than 30 years. Eric Sykes and Harry H. Corbett added a touch of glamour when they visited the company's premises in the 1960s.

The Hemel Hempstead and District Gas Company's works at Boxmoor, which are visible in the background, supplied the town's lighting at the turn of the century. The gas company produced about 30 million cubic feet of gas a year and had 700 customers.

Gaddesden Place.

Cheere House.

Heath Park.

Shendish House.

Gadebridge House.

Pendley Manor.

The Paper Empire

FOR nearly 200 years, the mills of John Dickinson were a mainstay of Dacorum's economic and social life. In fact, without this mini-industrial revolution in the Gade Valley, it is doubtful whether Hemel Hempstead would ever have become more than a small country town.

John Dickinson was born on 29 March 1782 – the eldest son of Captain Thomas Dickinson and his wife Francis. Having served an apprenticeship as a stationer, 15-year-old John was admitted to the Livery of the Stationers' Company in 1804 and started selling paper in the city.

Back then, paper was made by hand, sheet by sheet, but the quest to find a way of making a continuous roll of paper had begun.

Dickinson had already shown his inventiveness by producing a new kind of paper for cannon cartridges, which, unlike the paper ordinarily in use, did not smoulder and constantly cause accidental explosions. His invention was taken up by the army and used to good effect by the Duke of Wellington's men against Napoleon.

Henry Fourdriner became the first man continuously to manufacture paper – his first machine was not successful, but a second was erected and set to work at Frogmoor Mill.

But Dickinson was not far behind and in 1809, in partnership with the financier George Longman, he patented a new type of machine for producing paper – the 'endless web' – and bought Apsley Mill.

Soon after, he fell in love with Ann Grover, the daughter of a Hemel Hempstead solicitor and banker, and they were married a year later in 1810. Grover's father's bank, which eventually became part of Lloyds, helped Dickinson buy Nash Mills in 1811 and, a decade or so later, Home Park Mill and Croxley Mill.

Dickinson retired from the business in 1859 at the age of 77 and died at his home in London 10 years later, but the firm he had started went from strength to strength under the leadership of Charles Longman, Frederick Pratt Barlow and John Evans.

In 1886, Dickinson's became a private limited company which as well as the Hertfordshire mills and London office had by then expanded to include branches in Manchester, Bristol, Birmingham, Glasgow, Belfast, New York, Cape Town, Johannesburg, Durban, Bombay, Calcutta, Australia and New Zealand.

The output of the Hertfordshire mills in 1886 was about 200 tons of paper a week in addition to cards, envelopes and stationery.

The Railways

When John Dickinson came to Apsley in 1809 there were no trains, no buses, no cars – just horse-drawn transport that relied on muddy and rutted roads.

But the mill sites Dickinson chose had one great transport plus – the Grand Junction (no Union in those days) Canal.

By the turn of the century Dickinson kept a fleet of steam barges which each carried about 25 tons.

They brought coal and other materials to the mills and carried away paper and stationery. Every evening the boats left the mills at Apsley, Nash and Home Park and arrived in London at the company's warehouse, Irongate Wharf, Paddington, where they would unload their products for onward shipment around the country and the world.

But the railway began to take its grip in the 20th century as Dickinson's offices around the country grew. Even so, in 1938 the canal was still a major transport route for the mills.

By the 1930s, Dickinson's were in favour of letting the train take the strain and were instrumental in persuading the LMS to build Apsley Station which was opened on 22 September 1938.

The train may have got some extra passengers but the bus and bike remained the preferred transport for most employees and the A41 became a seething mass of humanity at the end of the working day as the buses queued to take the workers to their homes all around the district.

Apsley Mill

Apsley Mill, where it all started, began life as a corn mill belonging to the Abbey of St Albans.

By the time Dickinson's celebrated its centenary in 1904 very little of the old paper mill that John Dickinson bought in 1809 remained. In 1888, the manufacture of paper at Apsley stopped in favour of cards and envelopes.

The manufacture of card had begun there in 1831 and steadily increased so that by the turn of the century production was nearly 50 tons a week of everything from the finest ivory visiting cards to railway tickets. Envelope making was introduced in 1850 and the envelope machines gradually took up much of the space of the paper making plant.

In 1877 a special fireproof three-storey building was constructed for envelope production. In 1927 part of the old mill was demolished and a new envelope department built on the site.

By this time packaging envelopes for everything from sandwich bags to kippers were very much on the scene. In 1933 the mill produced 100 million envelopes in a week for the first time. A new building for the card department was constructed in 1933 for £100,000 and covered all that was left of Salmon Meadow. In the late 1930s Dickinson's had big plans to expand Apsley, but the war years intervened and the plans were never implemented.

In 1963 the new stationery factory opened on the Belswains Lane site and in 1982 Princess Michael of Kent opened the £6m DRG Stationery complex at Apsley after a major reorganisation. Then in 1988 came the idea of a giant new warehouse and plans to sell off part of the site to Sainsbury's.

Nash Mills

Nash Mills had already been converted from a corn mill when Dickinson bought it in 1811 and he found moulds for making paper by hand which dated back to 1797.

In 1813 a major part of the mill was destroyed by fire and Dickinson's house was only saved by hanging wet paper felts on the walls and roof. Damage done to the mill was put at £8,000, but it was rebuilt and in 1830

Dickinson installed his machine for making fine plate and Duplex papers.

In 1879 the mill was almost completely rebuilt with turbines replacing the old waterwheels and in 1888 electricity was used for the first time ever to drive one of the machines. At the turn of the century the mill housed the smiths', carpenters', and fitters' shops in which the machinery for all three mills was made and repaired.

Nash Mills was also the headquarters of the mills' fire brigade which was first set up in 1883. Nash Mills was not developed much during the early part of the 20th century, but in the 1920s new stores for raw materials, waste paper and wood pulp were built on the opposite side of the mill. Of the three mills in Dacorum it is Nash Mills that is set to go on booming into the new Millennium. In the sale of DRG, Nash Mills was acquired by Sappi and is now a thriving part of the local economy.

Home Park Mills

Home Park Mills were within the park that was attached to King Henry III's palace at Kings Langley.

The mill was built by John Dickinson in 1825 and enlarged in 1838, at which date it turned out 10 tons of paper each week.

In 1878 the first colouring machine was built at Nash Mills – prior to this all paper staining had been done by hand. The new machine was damaged by fire five years later, but this was repaired and the colouring expanded.

The mill underwent an entire change in 1888 when a large three-storey colouring mill was built with the water wheels being replaced by turbines. The early part of the 20th century saw a big increase in the demand for coloured paper and for a time a night shift was introduced at Kings Langley. Later in the century, gummed paper tapes were produced at Home Park Mills for use in packing and the product was known as Holdfast.

But sales nose-dived – possibly because DRG produced Sellotape at nearby Borehamwood – and in October 1989 the closure of the mills was announced with the loss of over 300 jobs. The mill, which stood on a site of about 18 acres, was sold the following year.

Apsley Mill at lunchtime.

Full steam ahead paper production.

Dickinson's factory in Nash Mills.

The man himself – John Dickinson.

An abiding memory for local people, as shown in these two pictures, whether they worked at the mills or not, is the scene on the A41 as it was then – London Road – at home time. Hundreds of workers spewed out on to the road and traffic was brought to a standstill until Dickinson's buses had left with the workers.

Home Park Mills in 1940.

Craftsmen at work in the book department of Dickinson's.

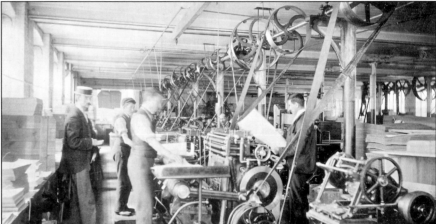

Women in Dickinson's machine room.

Bicycles were the mode of transport for most mill workers in the early 1930s, but the boss at Apsley naturally opted for a bit of a luxury.

Apsley Mills in the 1930s.

Transport Minister Leslie Burgen sees for himself how the company made use of the canal in the 1930s.

A Dickinson's lorry at Apsley Mills in the 1930s.

Staff in the post room in 1955.

The mills were full of complicated machinery.

The workers who made the paper and stationery and kept the mills going over the years were vital to the company, but equally important were those who sold the products. This picture shows the sales team in 1971.

Shendish House had a connection with John Dickinson's from the start – it was first built in 1856 by Charles Longman, a partner in the business. The company used to hold an annual sports and fun day there every June and it became one of the town's biggest events.

A company outing at Windsor.

Dickinson's barge – the Lord Nelson – by the Red Lion at the turn of the century.

Inside Dickinson's in the 1890s.

Men at work in Dickinson's at the turn of the century.

The machine room in the early 1900s.

Workers at Dickinson's on their daily exodus.

Dickinson's in Belswains Lane.

Workers enjoy an outing aboard one of the company's barges.

The company had its own rolling stock – for fun as well as serious uses.

The footbridge near Apsley Mills about 1900.

A steam barge leaving the mills.

Members of Dickinson's own fire brigade help celebrate a happy union between two of their colleagues.

Evacuees and Doodlebugs

WHAT hit Hemel Hempstead far more than German bombs at the start of World War Two was the arrival of 5,000 evacuees from the East End of London.

Billeting officers went round the town looking for accommodation for them and anyone who refused could be fined. Many local people were shocked by the state of the children which in some cases was so bad that clinics had to be set up to deal with problems such as nits, impetigo, sores and scabies.

The first trainload arrived at Boxmoor station on 1 December 1939 and consisted of evacuees and their teachers. Of the whole train load those youngsters who showed the slightest signs of tears could be counted on the fingers of one hand, the *Gazette* said. But this appears to have been rather a misleading viewpoint because afterwards there was so much bed-wetting by disturbed children that the WVS wrote a special leaflet on how to deal with the problem.

The report went on: 'Most of the evacuees carried a great deal of luggage, and some of the bags were almost as big as the little lads and lassies themselves, but they were helped by scouts and guides doing their good turn for evacuation day.'

Householders taking the evacuees were paid 10s (50p) for each child and those taking mothers and children had to provide sleeping accommodation and reasonable cooking facilities. For this they received 5s (25p) for the mother and 3s (15p) for her child.

There was quite a lot of local amazement at the evacuees and their reactions to being outside London for the first time. One lad shown a bed with white sheets shook his head and said he could not sleep there. When his host asked why, he replied: 'Well I sleep in the cupboard with father's coat over me at home.'

Emergency rations consisting of a tin of bully beef, biscuits, chocolate and a tin of condensed milk were given to each evacuee and it was intended that these should last them for 48 hours to avoid strain on the resources of local shops.

Once the children were established new problems started arising. In some cases schools catered for local children in the morning while in the afternoon they were taken over by the evacuees with their own teachers.

Saving and Rationing

There were no bombs, though, and the evacuees gradually began to drift away until by January 1940 over 80 per cent had returned home – only to come back when the London blitz started later in the year.

On the home front the war effort concentrated on savings to help pay for armaments, recycling, growing supplies and rationing to overcome shortages caused by the U-boats' blockade of our shores.

National Savings to raise money for warships and aircraft were an important part of the local war effort.

Food rationing came in January 1940, when each person was rationed to 4oz each of bacon, ham, butter and sugar. Clothes rationing and a new system of furniture rationing came a little later.

The first people to be hit by the war were motorists who were rationed for petrol and eventually there was no petrol at all for private motorists because so many tankers were being torpedoed by the Germans.

Among the new organisations set up was the Herts Herb Collecting Committee which collected rose hips for rose hip syrup, horse chestnuts for animal feeds, nettles for animal feeds and camouflage paint and poppy petals for cough mixture.

There was also great emphasis on salvage. Paper was collected for recycling, bones for glue and all food refuse had to be put aside to be collected for pig and poultry feed. As the war continued there was a shortage of many urgently needed metals and the Hemel Hempstead park gates were taken away to be melted down together with a large number of iron railings. Aluminium was badly needed for aircraft production and an appeal went round to everyone to hand in their aluminium pots and pans.

Other campaigns included Dig for Victory when all available land including front lawns was dug up and used to plant vegetables.

Dad's Army

Dacorum was many miles from the Channel coast, but there was still a need for security on the home front.

Parachutists were always a fear and if there was an invasion then the war could have come to local streets. Local people who were too old to serve in the armed forces, who didn't pass the medical examinations or who were engaged in valuable war work at home, joined the Home Guard instead.

Much of the Home Guard's training took place in Boxmoor and there were three ammunition shelters in Gadebridge Park. The rifle range in Piccotts End was used by American servicemen based at Bovingdon.

One of the weapons that the Home Guard had was the phosphorus bombs. In the latter days of the war some boys unearthed some of these and threw them into the River Gade and caused pandemonium. Although the Home Guard was for men, the women more than did their bit, working in factories and the Land Army helped on farms producing the crops that were so important for the nation.

War Work

The build-up to World War Two was a long one and one of the main fears for most people was of air raids and gas attacks.

A big fear was that bombing could lead to fire or that fires could be a signal to bombers, so regular firewatches were carried out. Gas masks were issued during the crisis of 1938 and trench shelters were also dug in many parts of Dacorum.

In local factories there was a great deal of activity as they switched over to war-time production.

Dickinson's, by far the largest employer in the area, gradually moved over to making munitions and by 1941 the Engineering Department was completely engaged in ammunition production while the Bankers Envelope Department was making shell containers. The Label Department was making tubes for shells and the Card Department TNT demolition cartons, while the Book Department was making mortar carriers and the Banker Department anti-aircraft shell containers.

Because of Dickinson's involvement in aircraft production the Apsley Mills section of the Home Guard was allocated two Lewis guns from early lease-lend supplies.

Dickinson's produced a massive amount of war material and was much involved in the Airgraph Service. This service speeded letters to and from the forces overseas and involved photographing and reducing a message written on a special form, then conveying it by air to destination points where it was enlarged, printed and delivered in a sealed envelope. The photographic work was done by Kodak at Harrow and Dickinson's made a machine which folded, printed the message, inserted it into an envelope which was printed, dated stamped and sealed in one operation, thus speeding up the operation. Dickinson's had dealt with 200 million airgraphs when the service was ended in July 1945.

Under bombardment

This area was never a target for the Germans, but it did experience bombing as the result of aircrew mistaking targets or wanting to get rid of their bombs after being damaged.

The worst bombing incident during the war in Hemel Hempstead took place on a moonlit night on 10 May 1941, when a bomb fell on Belswains Lane and destroyed two houses and killed nine people.

Towards the end of the war came the flying bombs – 'doodlebugs' – aimed at London. Several landed in Dacorum, but no one was killed or injured by them.

In Hemel Hempstead a total of 90 high explosive devices landed in the town. Nine failed to explode – seven were detonated by the bomb disposal squad while two were taken away. Four oil bombs, one flying bomb and about 350 incendiary devices also fell within the borough during World War Two.

The Home Guard in Northchurch.

The crew of the submarine *United* visited Berkhamsted and presented the town with a Jolly Roger during the war.

One big fear during World War Two was that bombing could lead to a huge fire, so regular firewatches were carried out. Our picture shows men on duty at Dickinson's in Apsley.

Dickinson's, by far the largest employer in the area, gradually moved over to making munitions and by 1941 the engineering department was completely engaged in making ammunition production while the bankers envelope department was making shells.

Many women took part in war work at Dickinson's and by early 1944 around 130 women were working in two requisitioned garages in Berkhamsted.

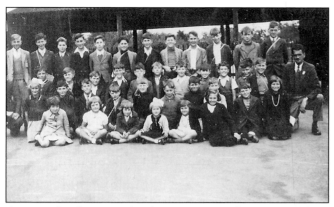

Scores of refugees arrived in Dacorum during World War Two. This group of about 40 children arrived at Boxmoor Station before being bussed to homes in Bovingdon. They were incorporated into the village school then graduated to Corner Hall School in Hemel Hempstead.

Members of the Inns of Court Training Regiment relaxing while on manoeuvres near Berkhamsted. The regiment paraded through the town on Armistice Day chanting: 'We've won the bloody war.' And, right, a soldier on manoeuvres near Gadebridge Park, Hemel Hempstead.

Dickinson's own branch of the Home Guard.

Because of Dickinson's involvement in aircraft production, the Apsley Mills section of the Home Guard was given two Lewis guns from early lease-lend suppliers and draped in camouflage.

The Home Guard on the roof of Dickinson's.

The devastation in Belswains Lane the day after the bombs fell.

The Home Guard – looking suspiciously like the cast of *Dad's Army* – practising manoeuvres on Boxmoor.

A mock tank being towed on to Boxmoor.

Evacuees had a greater impact on Dacorum than the occasional rain of bombs.

Residents in Queen Street, Hemel Hempstead, celebrate VE day.

VE day prompted rejoicing across the borough – like this party in Herbert Street, Hemel Hempstead.

A sit-down celebration on VE day in the High Street, Hemel Hempstead.

For those who've moved into the area in the last 20 or 30 years it must be difficult to appreciate that Bovingdon was once home to an important wartime airfield and nearly became a main airport for London. The files of the *Gazette* for the period after World War Two have many references to Bovingdon Airfield, but wartime censorship meant the paper could not report on some of the airfield's most dramatic times. Bovingdon, though, played a big part in securing supremacy in the sky during World War Two.

In his book *Hertfordshire and Bedfordshire Airfields*, historian Graham Smith says: 'Without doubt Bovingdon would have been an aircraft spotter's paradise during the wartime years – no other Eighth Airforce base housed such a wide variety of American wartime aircraft.'

The airfield was constructed in 1941-2 for the RAF but allocated to the USAF before it opened. Mainly a

training and operational crew supply base, Bovingdon was called upon to mount some missions, the first in October 1942 when 24 B-17s took part in a raid on a steelworks at Lille.

Most of the VIPs who came from across the Atlantic to visit Britain arrived at Bovingdon, including the stars who came to entertain the American servicemen and women – Bob Hope, Bing Crosby, Clark Gable, Marlene Dietrich and Glenn Miller. General Dwight Eisenhower's personal B-17 was based at Bovingdon during the time he was Supreme Allied Commander in Europe.

Bovingdon was a very high profile base. It was a major staging post for aircraft returning to the USA and in 1943 the *Memphis Belle* left Bovingdon to fly back to the States for a war-bond raising tour of the country. When the war ended Bovingdon became well used as a freight and as a passenger airport. There were many mishaps, with planes overshooting the runway and ending up in Chesham Road quite a regular occurrence.

It finally closed as an airfield in 1972. Soon afterwards the first suggestion of a prison on the site was made, although sheep moved in first. Today the prison, The Mount, has been accepted as a fixture, but there is still controversy over what use the rest of the airfield should be put to.

More memories of Bovingdon Airfield in these four pictures.

Before the New

AT THE beginning of 1947, the residents of Hemel Hempstead already knew that their town was being considered as the site for one of three new towns around London, but no decisions had been made.

But what was Hemel Hempstead like in 1947? If you were coming into town to do your shopping you would have boarded the bus, but it is very unlikely you would have had a car.

The bus would have taken you to the terminus in Bury Road – now the bottom stretch of Queensway. The land now occupied by the college was a commercial and residential area and the River Gade that flows at the back of the town centre had watercress beds rather than today's familiar Water Gardens.

There were shops in Marlowes, but nothing like the numbers of today and there were plenty of plush houses too, some of which survive as office accommodation.

Today the 'Magic Roundabout' has become something of a landmark, but there was no roundabout of any description in those days: the junction of Marlowes, Two Waters Road, Station Road and Wood Lane was just a crossroads!

Leighton Buzzard Road did not exist, either – if you wanted to get to Marlowes, Cotterells was your only route. Your route to St Albans would have been down Lawn Lane and up St Albans Road – now known as St Albans Hill – which was a single carriageway road, not today's high speed dual carriageway.

If you were off to Leighton Buzzard you would have cycled out through Piccotts End. There was no road through the park, which in those days was overlooked by Gadebridge House. Warners End – then better known as Counters End – Gadebridge, Bennett's End, Highfield, Grovehill, Chaulden were mainly fields and open countryside. Woodhall Farm was the site of a Brocks firework factory. Boxmoor, Leverstock Green, Apsley and Piccotts End were already well established, but were regarded in many ways as separate villages.

'Everyone knew Everyone'

By far the largest employer in the town was John Dickinson – the paper and stationery manufacturer – and just about every family had someone or knew someone who worked at the mills.

For entertainment there was very little in the way of television, but the pictures were popular. In January 1947 you could have gone to the Luxor (telephone Boxmoor 36 for times) and seen Roy Rogers and Dale Evans in *Sunset In Eldorado* or to the Princess (Boxmoor 106) to catch *Blossoms In The Dust*, which featured Greer Garson and Walter Pidgeon. Both the Princess and Luxor were in Marlowes.

If you were going out of town you had a choice of railway lines. Boxmoor Station, now known as Hemel Hempstead, was the most popular starting point for a trip to London. But the Nicky Line which ran to Redbourn and connected up with the main line through Luton to London was still in operation and there were sidings in Cotterells.

Many people who lived in the town in those days say it was a community in which 'everyone knew everyone'.

Perhaps – but it may surprise some to know that the population of Hemel Hempstead back in 1947 was still over 20,000, a sizeable town and bigger than today's Berkhamsted.

A stretch of the canal alongside Bourne End Mill.

The Lloyds building at the entrance to the High Street in the early 1940s.

The staff of International Stores in the High Street with the entrance of Hemel Hemstead Engineering works to the right of those premises.

The long-serving employees of Hemel Hempstead Engineering in the 1930s.

Santa does the rounds in Tring in 1940.

Berkhamsted in the snow before World War Two.

Berkhamsted High Street in 1947.

A day out in the 1940s.

Marlowes in the late 1940s/early 1950s.

At the turn of the century, Marlowes looked very different to how it does now. This picture shows the old Henry VIII pub and the perambulator hire shop to the right.

At one time, the borough was blessed with Co-ops.
People in Hemel Hempstead, Berkhamsted and Tring all boasted their own shops.

It was still "All at the Co-op" in these pages of shops and delivery vehicles.

The staff of Kingham and Sons in the High Street, Hemel Hempstead and the store's interior.

Ramsey MacDonald, Britain's first-ever Labour Prime Minister, cut the first sod for the town's Labour Hall in Wood Lane in 1928. All the town's Labour stalwarts turned out to hear Mr MacDonald's 'inspiring speech'. In fact, it was so inspiring that the hall was completed using voluntary labour in less than a year.

First sod being cut by Ramsey MacDonald, seen in the centre of the group on the right.

Boxmoor's Stan Snoxall driving a 1904 Humber single cylinder car in the London to Brighton vintage car run in the late 1940s. His father, Frederick Snoxall, was a chauffeur at Lockers Park in Hemel Hempstead. He drove a 1908 Minerva.

Hemel Hempstead Grammar School, described as a 'modern interpretation of English Renaissance of the late 17th century' by its architect, opened in 1931. The first class, pictured here, enjoyed a wealth of facilities including an assembly room, physics and chemistry labs and a gym and library.

This fatal accident at Tring Station in 1903 was one of many crashes that blighted the railway in the first few decades of the 20th century.

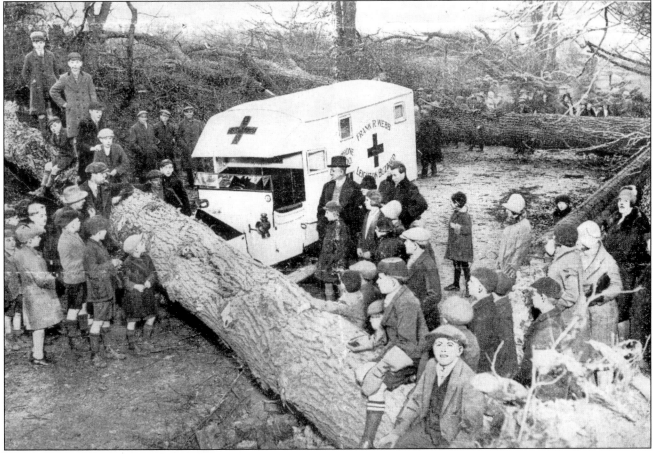

The great gale of 1930 blew down scores of trees – one of which crashed on to this ambulance as it passed along Gadebridge Lane. Miraculously, no one was killed. 15 trees fell in Piccotts End Road alone and thousands turned out to see the damage the following day.

The licensee of the Bell Hotel in the High Street, Hemel Hempstead, had a lucky escape when a brick lorry crashed through the hotel's front window in 1949.

People were protesting about the noise nuisance from Midland Station at the dawn of the 20th century. It was caused by shunting that was carried out at night so things could be speeded up in the mornings.

The Apsley bell ringers set off on their annual outing in 1928.

Unveiling the Master Plan

THE idea of new towns had been around before World War Two – Letchworth and Welwyn Garden City, also in Hertfordshire. But after World War Two the pace stepped up.

New Homes

The new town was mainly about new homes for Londoners, but in Hemel Hempstead itself there was plenty of need for new homes for local people.

As servicemen returned from the war the need for housing grew and grew. There were 1,600 families on the housing waiting list in Hemel Hempstead and the situation was so bad that 'squatting' in empty buildings, while not openly encouraged, had support from many quarters.

In July 1946 the post-war Labour government announced that it was considering Hemel Hempstead as the site of a new town – Satellite Town No 3 – in accordance with the government's 'policy for the decentralisation of persons and industry from London'.

Initially, the reaction to the minister's proposals did not appear hostile. But things quickly went sour as people realised that if the new town proposal was confirmed it would be carried out by a government-appointed development corporation, not the town's council, and that existing homes and businesses could well find themselves compulsorily purchased to make way for new developments.

By the autumn of 1946 opposition was mounting. Anti-new town candidates stood at local elections and a Hemel Hempstead Protection Association was formed.

The *Gazette* made its own position on the new town very clear. The following, from October 1946, is just one of many similar page one editorials that the *Gazette* carried over the coming three years: 'The new town plan, which if proceeded with will irrecoverably alter the character of Hemel Hempstead from a semi-rural township to a series of ungainly industrial sprawls overflowing from one valley to the other, looms large on our immediate horizon.'

New Town

The first plan of the new town of Hemel Hempstead was unveiled in September 1947.

What did it consist of? There was the central area, the industrial area largely in the vicinity of Cupid Green, and seven residential areas based on Hammerfield, Counters End, Warners End, Grovehill, Adeyfield, Leverstock Green and Apsley.

Much emphasis was placed on open spaces. In the central area, the High Street would be retained, but Marlowes was to be totally redeveloped – as a sort of modern promenade, after the fashion of Cheltenham or Princes Street, Edinburgh – and the area to the east was to be totally redeveloped in secluded architectural squares and terraces.

Looking at what we now know as the Marlowes area, a new civic centre, with council offices and assembly hall, was to be built at the Gadebridge Park end. Together with a large lake behind it, it would take up a goodish chunk of Gadebridge Park.

At the other end of Marlowes a boating lake adjacent to Heath Park was planned. Between this and the Civic Centre would be the Water Gardens with the Gade winding backwards and forwards, splitting the gardens into sections.

At each end of the gardens would be a car park, one of which would later be used as a helicopter landing strip. Cultural buildings, including two theatres, a library, art gallery and restaurant would be spaced out in the gardens. The shopping centre would be along a new Marlowes which would only be open to buses, with pedestrian access from the Water Gardens by means of underpasses.

The western slopes of the valley overlooking the town centre would contain lines of terraces in the manner of those at Clifton and Bath. Away from the central area, Boxmoor and Apsley railway stations would be closed down and a new station built at Two Waters. There would be an inner circular road and an outer bypass.

The new town opponents, the *Gazette* prominent among them, were not impressed: 'To most residents of this historic borough it may seem a colossal planned nightmare from some fevered imagination, but who could possibly grudge the erection of a suitable monument to a party (clearly a big dig at the Labour government of the time) which seems so determined to immolate itself on the altars of planned long-term imbecility?'

Work on the new town began in earnest in April 1949 when Mayor of Hemel Hempstead Councillor A.L. Selden laid a stone to mark the start of work on the first new town house.

This was in Adeyfield at the corner of what was to become Longlands and Homefield Road. Performing the ceremony, which was covered by BBC radio and photographed for television, the mayor referred to the 'mixed feelings' there had been and were over the new town and pointed out that no great accomplishment was ever achieved without some form of revolution: 'Even the votes for women caused quite a stir and a sensation and I would liken the new town in similar fashion as something that takes getting used to, and we should get used to it in a kindly manner.'

On the same day, the development corporation held an exhibition at Greenhills to show models of the houses to be built in the first stage of Adeyfield. These included what the *Gazette* described as a 'sensation' – a 10-storey skyscraper block of flats.

Another bit of news causing much comment early in 1949 was the Labour government's proposals to nationalise pubs in new towns. Local publicans were horrified. Thankfully, it never happened.

The 'Final Plan'

Everyone was waiting for what was described as the 'Final Plan' for the town from the development corporation.

The plan was unveiled in August 1949 – the same week as many people living in the town centre received notice that the development corporation were applying for a compulsory purchase order affecting their land. There were modifications to the plan, but few surprises, said the *Gazette*. The development of the town centre had been broken down into smaller plans so that the overall redevelopment would take place over a longer period. It was envisaged that in 18 months' time house construction would reach 600 a year.

The *Gazette* reported that there was 'general relief' at the modifications, but the relief didn't last very long.

In October Hemel Hempstead Borough Council voted to appeal to the government to put an end to the development of the new town and a little later in the month the Hemel Hempstead Protection Association declared the master plan an 'utter failure' at a crowded public meeting in St John's Hall. The borough council tried hard to get the development corporation to say what the estimated cost of the new town would be but the corporation refused. However, Councillor K. Dunkley, carried out 'weeks of hard effort' and came up with a figure of at least £55,446,000.

The public inquiry into the master plan opened in November and the development corporation faced a barrage of criticism.

It wasn't all bad vibes though. Councillor Gilbert Hitchcock welcomed the scheme on behalf of the trades council, which represented some 1,800 trades unionists in the town, and also on behalf of the Labour party. He thought the new town would provide greater opportunities for young people. The inquiry lasted for five days and the final decision was down to the government.

The First Families

The first four families of Hemel Hempstead's new town moved into their homes at Adeyfield in February 1950.

First to arrive were Mr and Mrs J. Ellerby of Derby Avenue, Harrow Weald, with their two children. This was the first time they had their own home in 15 years of married life and, despite the mud which constituted their garden and the building work all around, Mr and Mrs Ellerby were 'overjoyed' with their house.

Mr and Mrs B. Adams were next to arrive. They came from Wembley and had been living in rooms. Mr and Mrs S.G. Neal with their three children had been living in a three-roomed flat in Acton and Mr and Mrs R. Fee, the fourth family, had been living with their in-laws in Willesden.

They were greeted by a posse of VIPs including the Mayor, Councillor White, Lord Reith, the chairman of the development corporation, officials from various councils and Sir Thomas Sheepshanks, the permanent secretary at the Ministry of Town and Country Planning.

In welcoming them, Councillor White asked them to have patience as the town might seem 'a little dreary' at the moment. In the summer it would be very different, he promised: 'The people of Hemel Hempstead are not so bad when you get to know them. They are sound happy people and once you know them you are assured of their friendship. In three months' time when the chestnut trees are out, when the hawthorns are in bloom and the may is in the hedges, and when you see the bluebells in the wood, you will say there is no lovelier spot in England than Hemel Hempstead.'

Creating Work

With the arrival of the first new 'townies', attention focused on the local jobs situation. The year began with local employers warning that the labour shortages at existing firms would absorb an extra 2,000 workers and if work on new town factories began a 'serious position might arise'.

The development corporation took a different view and general manager Mr W.O. Hart warned that if the factory building programme was delayed Hemel Hempstead could become a dormitory town.

The first factory to be opened in the new town was, in fact, an established local business. In June 1950, the new works of the Hemel Hempstead Engineering Company, formerly based in the High Street, were opened at Cupid Green.

The master plan for the new town was finally approved by Mr Hugh Dalton, Minister of Town and Country Planning, following a visit that month.

One of the the major decisions the minister made that was to have – and still has – a major impact on the town was to back the development corporation's decision to put the town centre at the southern end of Marlowes.

Hemel Hempstead Borough Council had urged that the centre should be at the northern end, around the bottom of the High Street, with a link between the two and the borough engineer, Mr A.H. Turner, had prepared plans for such a proposal. The council feared that the old town would suffer if the new developments were away from the High Street.

Promoting the New Town

Portraying the new town to prospective residents in London was causing concern to the development corporation.

In 1950 they decided to make a film – to be called *A Home of Your Own* – which would be shown as part of the 1951 Festival of Britain.

But many people felt the film would just be propaganda. The Hemel Hempstead Council of Social Service was involved in helping with the film and Councillor Mayo, that body's chairman, had to issue a statement saying that if the film did contain propaganda it had nothing to do with them.

Things got so bad that in November, Hemel Hempstead Borough Council actually debated the film and passed a resolution that it would not support or participate in the project. But film making continued and by the time *A Home of Your Own* had its premiere, feelings had mellowed – the *Gazette* even said it made an 'excellent impression'.

In June, Hemel Hempstead's exhibition for the Festival of Britain opened at 149 Marlowes. It was a joint venture between Hemel Hempstead Borough Council and the development corporation. It was designed to show the town's past, present and future. Visitors were expected from all over the world and sightseeing trips of Hemel Hempstead were arranged for every Friday. Visitors were met at the station, taken on a bus tour of the town and the 5s cost included a cup of tea.

A fleet of vans ready to roll at Lyons Bakery depot.

The first family – the Ellerbys – move into the new town.

The Rotax site, soon to be better known as the home of Lucas Aerospace, as work began in the early 1950s. The other picture (below) shows the completed factory.

The cavernous factory of the London Ferro Concrete company, which made pre-fabricated concrete sections for building more factories.

meet the A-M family

This family of business machines and systems enjoys an international reputation for cutting costs in the field of addressing, copying, duplicating and printing, cold-type composing, and data processing. There's scarcely a business in the world that can't profit from using A-M highly practical machines and methods. These you should know about because they incorporate the know-how and expertise of forty years experience in mechanising paperwork procedures. For more information on any member of our talented family write to :-

ADDRESSOGRAPH-MULTIGRAPH LTD.,
HEMEL HEMPSTEAD, HERTS.
TEL: HEMEL HEMPSTEAD 2251

Addressograph
Multilith
Bruning
VariTyper

Office machinery specialists Addressograph-Multigraph's factory and one of their marvellous machines, shown in the advertisement, right.

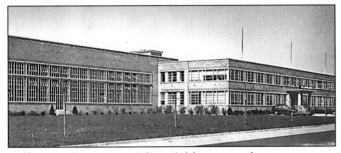

Multicore Solders, one of the few original firms still based on Maylands Avenue.

The first premises of the British Standards Institute, which still has offices in Hemel Hempstead.

The Bartlett's works on Maylands Avenue, back in the days when it still had a chimney.

The first shops on Maylands Avenue take shape.

Reliance Rubber became the largest manufacturer of moulded seamless hot water bottles in the world – producing an astonishing 1.5 million a year.

Access Equipment specialised in adjustable, mobile working platforms for all sorts of maintenance jobs.

Alford & Alder, a motor vehicle engineering company, came to Hemel Hempstead in 1952.

Willie Samuel, the managing director of Central Tool, casts an approving eye over a model of his new factory.

Marlowes being resurfaced outside the *Gazette* offices in 1949.

This now unfamiliar street scene from the 1950s shows Marlowes, including the Salvation Army Hall and the Post Office, before the new town revolution took hold.

Men at work in Hemel Hempstead Engineering's factory at Cupid Green. The firm, whose roots go right back to 1798, moved into the former offices of the Ministry of Supply in 1948 – below, an original artist's impression of what the new town centre would look like.

Harry Locke and some of the other stars from Hemel Hempstead Development Corporation's film *A Home Of Your Own*. The film, made to be shown at the 1951 Festival of Britain, irritated the Hemel Hempstead Protection Association who felt it would not show enough of the old town.

Below: A view of the steel houses taken in 1950. In this picture, work is starting on Maylands School.

Minister of Housing and Local Government Harold Macmillan laid the foundation stone of the Rotax (later Lucas) factory in January 1952.

The Square – later to become Queen's Square – takes shape in 1951.

Mayor of Hemel Hempstead A.L. Selden lays a stone to mark the start of work on the first house in 1949.

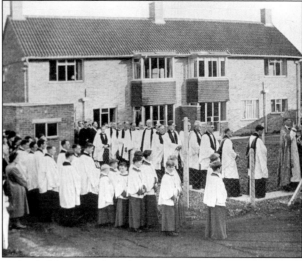

Adeyfield Free Church was not really a church at all – it was a garage. In the absence of a proper church, the Bishop of St Albans blessed the garage in the name of St Faith.

Thomas Coram School in Berkhamsted became Ashlyns School in 1951.

The new town's first four houses in Homefield Road nearing completion.

Royal Appointment, Human Sacrifice

In a little under two years, the development corporation had placed contracts for 886 houses, of which nearly 200 were complete and 150 occupied.

By the end of 1951, 1,000 houses were finished and work on the town centre would start by the next autumn.

Up until 1951, the new town revolution had been confined to Adeyfield, but towards the end of the year work started on Bennetts End.

In fact, work progressed so well on Bennetts End that Messrs Leslie & Co of Kensington, who were building a large number of flats and houses, bought barrels of beer that Christmas and the site foreman served pints to bricklayers and labourers on Christmas Eve. This was also the year that saw the beginnings on paper of Chaulden and Warners End.

In July 1951 the development corporation issued compulsory purchase notices for large tracts of land in the area including 'a parcel of approximately 8,341 acres situated on the west side of a cartway known as Grassy Bottom, Hemel Hempstead'.

The corporation explained that because of the successful development of the new industrial area where several large factories would be completed by the following year, it would be necessary to press on with its housing programme. The Apsley/Bennetts End area would not provide sufficient housing sites for more than the 1952-3 seasons and a start would be made on the western side of the town in the spring of 1953.

The area to the north of Chaulden Lane from Bargrove Avenue and Hammerfield to the edge of the designated area was about 730 acres and the population forecasts from the development corporation were: Boxmoor, up from 3,960 to 6,690; Chaulden, up from 170 to 5,300; Warners End, up from 44 to 6,050.

The Queen Visits

The visit of Her Majesty the Queen to Hemel Hempstead in July 1952 was welcomed by supporters and opponents of the new town.

She had originally agreed to come to lay the foundation stone for the new church in Adeyfield – it was to become St Barnabas – while she was still Princess Elizabeth, but the death of her father, King George VI, on 6 February, had meant there were fears the visit would not take place – fears that were put to rest in April 1952.

Preparations for the royal visit went on for weeks. It's interesting to note that despite the great opposition to the demolition of buildings in Marlowes one building, the Marlowes Bridge, which carried the Nicky Line was described as 'a ghastly sight'.

It was decided to hide it from Her Majesty by festooning it with flowers and foliage provided by the Hemel Hempstead Townswomen's Guild, and Leverstock Green and Felden WIs. Labour would be provided by the Hemel Hempstead Manufacturers Association and the Fire Brigade.

Crowds began gathering along the route early in the morning. The borough council provided seats for as many elderly people as possible and the crowd gathered at the Plough junction was estimated to be over 1,000. Schoolchildren in their uniforms also lined parts of the route despite the heat of the day. There were over 2,000 in The Square to watch the Queen lay the foundation stone.

After the ceremony the Queen went on a tour of the new town areas and stopped at the homes of the first four residents. She was to have gone into the home of the first tenants, the Ellerby family, but five-year-old Dennis Ellerby had gone down with chicken pox and to prevent a royal 'itch' mum Daisy Ellerby had to watch from her window as Her Majesty visited the home of the neighbouring Adams family. The Adams' now had four children and the Queen met them as well as nine-year-old Beverley's goldfish. Before Her Majesty left, Mrs Adams offered her a cup of tea. Two weeks after her visit the Queen sent a letter thanking the people of Adeyfield for the flowers.

'Seeking to Devour…'

The year the Queen visited Hemel Hempstead may be thought of as the year that Hemel Hempstead new town was universally recognised as 'being on the map.'

But 1952 was also the year in which opposition to the new town was at its most vehement – even compared to the first days of 1947. It began with the tragic case of the widow who died of a 'broken heart' because the new town took her home. In consecutive weeks of front page editorials the *Gazette* told the story of the widow who had been forced to leave her home in the town centre's Bridge Street after it was compulsorily purchased by the development corporation. She was, said the *Gazette*, 'a human sacrifice to the Metropolitan Moloch which reaches its covetous fingers out over the green countryside seeking whom or what it may devour'.

Lessons Learnt

One of the early new town problems was a chronic shortage of school places. The post war economic crisis had meant money for new schools was in short supply and the new Conservative government that came to power in 1951 had put an embargo on new buildings until the spring of 1952. For the new town of Hemel Hempstead, with new children now arriving almost daily, the problem was getting critical.

In the spring of 1952, Labour organised a meeting at Maylands School – the only new town school then completed. One mother complained her child had no paper to draw on and it was said that 31 per cent of all classes had more than 40 children. In Adeyfield, some children were being taught in huts and canteens and Maylands School, which was intended for primary school children,

was catering for some of secondary age. Children from the new town area were being transported to schools that could fit them in.

On the brighter side, the first new town pub – the New Venture – opened on Boxing Day. The powers that be had already decided that the number of pubs in Hemel Hempstead before the new town would still be sufficient for expanded population, so the opening sounded the death knell for two pubs – the Saracen's Head in Adeyfield and the Halfway House in Marlowes.

Another new public amenity was Gadebridge Park. The Gadebridge Estate was owned by Sir Astley Paston Cooper. Gadebridge House itself was a school, but Sir Astley made the decision to sell after the development corporation's plans for Warners End were made public. Warners End would swallow up hundreds of acres of the estate – mostly farm land including Home Farm – but virtually excluded the part known as Gadebridge Park.

The council decided to buy the park in three stages – the first being the area behind the High Street and the second an area stretching south from Gadebridge Lane to the iron bridge. All 100 acres would cost the council a total of £14,500, it was reported. The second part was bought in 1953, and the school and its grounds, where new houses stand now, was fenced off. The public park was 'christened' with its first event in February 1953 – a race in the snow between Hemel Hempstead Cycling club on their bikes and Greenhills Athletics Club's runners.

Bennett's End

As autumn approached the focus switched from the growth of Adeyfield to the birth of Bennetts End. The first residents moved in during the summer and by the end of November around 300 houses were occupied – but there were no facilities and no bus service.

The residents only had one shop – the converted sitting room of a house in Candlefield Road. The shop was run by Mr Smith, who had come from Finchley and three assistants. He stocked provisions, hardware, confectionery, cigarettes and postage stamps.

In a new year message for 1953, Alderman Mayo who was chairman of the Hemel Hempstead Council of Social Service, said he believed the development of the town centre would help unify old and new. He said: "Even its greatest admirers could never pretend Hemel Hempstead offers much in the way of shopping facilities apart from the ordinary requirements of everyday life."

Leverstock Green

During the first six years of the new town Leverstock Green had remained relatively untouched, but in the summer of 1953 the development corporation told residents that the population of the village was to be raised from 1,000 to 3,000.

The green was to be enlarged to approximately twice its size and one side of the green would be used for 'working class' homes, although these would 'be a better type than those at Adeyfield'.

There would be a 'middle class' residential area where plots of land would be for sale and the old school, which many residents described as attractive, would have to be demolished.

In addition, the borough council published plans for 980 new dwellings in what was to be Highfield, but work didn't start until September 1954.

Another new development on the horizon was a grammar school in Bennetts End. Herts County Council unveiled plans for the 612 place school which would cost £198,334, but some councillors demanded a rethink on expenditure for sculptures described as 'monstrosities'.

Gurton's Stores, which used to deliver goods by motorcycle combination in the 1920s, was compulsorily purchased for the new town development in 1952.

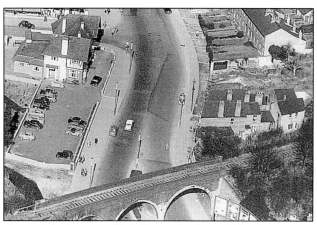

An aerial picture of Marlowes in the 1950s shows the site of the old Waggon and Horses pub near the railway arch, which was replaced by the new Waggon and Horses in the 1930s. That, too, has long since disappeared.

These two pictures show Marlowes in 1951 and 1952. The Parade has not changed that much, although many of the shops and businesses have gone. The other side of Marlowes is now West Herts College. The second picture shows what stood on the site of the Full House pub. You can see the Co-op, the Princess Cinema and the public baths.

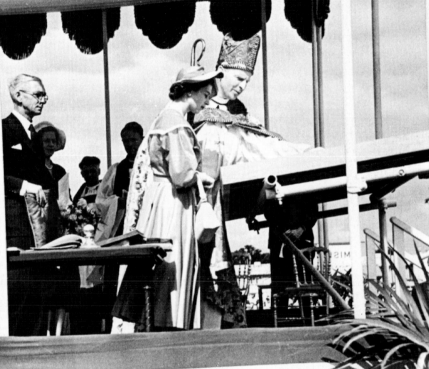

Both supporters and opponents of the new town welcomed the visit of Her Majesty the Queen to Hemel Hempstead on Sunday 20 July 1952. She had originally come to lay the foundation stone for the new church in Adeyfield – it was to become St Barnabas – while she was still Princess Elizabeth, but the death of her father King George VI on 6 February had prompted fears the visit would not take place – fears that were put to rest on 1 April that year. The people showed their appreciation by lining the streets for her visit and cheering.

Bennetts End boasted a single shop in 1952 – and even that occupied a converted sitting room in Candlefield Road. The shop stocked provisions, hardware, confectionery, cigarettes and postage stamps.

Chaulden House was within the area of compulsory purchase for the new neighbourhood of Chaulden.

Above and right: Work begins on Bennetts End and Bennettsgate in 1953.

Above and right: The road layout of Boxted Road, Long Chaulden and Northridge Way in Warners End in 1953. The *Gazette* said: 'The streets may not be paved with gold, but the neat rows of houses in Hemel Hempstead's new western neighbourhoods of Chaulden sparkle in the sun as fresh and bright as a new pin.'

It's known as the 'Magic Roundabout' and it's famous around the world. In 1947, when it was announced that Hemel Hempstead was to become a new town, what we know today as the Magic Roundabout at the entrance to the town centre was little more than a road junction between Station Road, Wood Lane, Lawn Lane and Marlowes.

There was no dual carriageway and traffic at that time was light. But as the new town came traffic grew and by 1953 the Ministry of Transport came up with a £5,000 temporary scheme for a roundabout. In 1955 a scheme for a roundabout was agreed which would involve the demolition of the Plough pub. The roundabout eventually opened in 1956, but it was much different from the busy Magic Roundabout of today which is known throughout the world.

It wasn't until the 1970s that traffic volumes had increased so much that it became clear something would have to be done to ease the congestion and the Magic Roundabout was born. Work began on a scheme which would incorporate six mini-roundabouts in early 1973 and the new look roundabout was opened as an experiment in June.

Its opening attracted the national press and television and the *Gazette* reported it caused some of the biggest traffic jams ever seen in Hemel Hempstead. It was the first such roundabout anywhere and it quickly eased the town's traffic problems.

It had been an experiment, but within a year it had been agreed to make it permanent and the people of the town soon took it to their hearts. Such was the feeling for the roundabout and its success that in the 1990s when some traffic experts suggested that traffic lights should replace it, the *Gazette* launched a Save Our Roundabout campaign with stickers and a mass petition.

More memories of the Magic Roundabout in these three pictures.

Berkhamsted Place was demolished more than 30 years ago after it fell into a state of terminal disrepair.

The Faltering Heart

A FORETASTE of the problems the new town centre would inflict on the old town came in October 1953 when the town's bus terminus was moved from Bury Road.

Its new home was a temporary one opposite Hillfield Road – the terminus we know today was not completed for another two years – and the move was necessary because of road works.

London Transport failed to provide passengers with any shelter, but of more long term significance was the effect the switch would have on the High Street. It meant there were no buses serving the old town, apart from a two-hourly service from Gaddesden and some from Adeyfield.

A letter in the *Gazette* signed by a large number of traders said: 'A High Street without a bus service is like a heart with the main artery blocked and, if the blood supply is not speedily restored, then the heart ceases to function.'

Changing Politics

As the town changed, so did its politics. The Hemel Hempstead Borough Council had been a mixture of independent and Conservative councillors with Labour on the fringes.

By 1954 the influx of Londoners, regarded mainly as Labour voters, was playing a very significant part in the make up of the chamber. The parties geared up to woo the 2,500 new voters in the borough council elections of 1954, at which eight council seats were up for grabs.

The elections produced a big gain for Labour – they took three seats from the Conservatives and two from the Ratepayers' Association. The election left the two parties at nine seats each and Labour's Gilbert Hitchcock had high hopes of being elected Hemel Hempstead's first ever Labour Mayor. In those days the council also included six aldermen – three were Conservative and Councillor Hitchcock had to wait two years before being elected mayor.

But the wind of change was blowing strongly and when the following year's general election came Labour was out in force. One of the party's great national figures, Nye Bevan, came to speak at Adeyfield School in support of local candidate Norman MacKenzie. More than 800 people heard him speak.

The election a few days later brought an 83 per cent turnout but Hemel Hempstead's long-serving Conservative MP, Lady Frances Davidson – who had wide respect throughout the constituency – was again the victor. She was the town's MP from 1937 to 1959.

Employment Boom

The failure to meet the schooling needs of the rapidly growing population of the new town was a continuing theme of the early years.

Mr Hart, general manager of the development corporation, made it clear he was not happy with the provision of schools: only four were under construction in the spring of 1954 – Hobbs Hill Wood, Chambersbury, Chaulden and another primary school for Adeyfield.

Elsewhere, things were progressing nicely: Gadebridge made its first appearance on the drawing board in 1954, work was under way on several more new factories in Maylands Avenue and the borough was experiencing its 'biggest ever employment boom'. There were just 107 registered unemployed people, but only 21 of them had been unemployed for more than eight weeks.

Halfway Stage

The new town as originally envisaged in 1947 reached its halfway stage in 1955: 4,732 houses had been built, 2,000 were under construction and the population had risen from 21,200 in 1947 to 38,700.

Although much had been done, there was continuing concern from many quarters that the provision of vital facilities such as schools, hospitals and social infrastructure – community centres, playing fields, bus services – was nowhere near keeping pace with the construction of houses.

The exodus from the old town was becoming a torrent. In August the town's courthouse, which had been based at the Town Hall for 400 years, moved out to a temporary home in Boxmoor Hall with plans to move on to a new home in the town centre in the future.

Bridge Street was beginning to rise from the rubble of the old and work also started on the £41,000 extension to Midland Road to link it with Marlowes.

There was a new look to the entrance to Gadebridge Park as the old air raid shelters were demolished and a 200-year-old Canadian pine felled to give an unrestricted view of the Charter Tower.

The first of Hemel Hempstead's town centre sculptures also made its appearance in November 1955. *The Four Stages of the Development of Man* by Professor A.H. Gerrard of the Slade School of Fine Arts was unveiled by Dame Evelyn Sharp. The four panels can still be seen on the wall of a shop on the corner of Bridge Street and Marlowes. The cost of the sculpture was £2,000, which provoked many letters to the *Gazette* complaining about the 'waste of public money'.

New Industry

By the middle of 1955 there were 22 factories in production on the new industrial area and five more were under construction.

Just under 4,000 people were employed at the factories and there was much diversification – from Alford & Alder and its engineering to the Reliance Rubber Co with its hot water bottles and the J. Lyons food storage depot.

Interest in the arrival on the scene of commercial television – was causing problems in the town. The council was concerned that a rash of new aerials to receive the new ITV station would make the town look unsightly, but the development corporation agreed that their tenants could put up aerials. Eventually, in September 1955, the council decided to give the OK. But by then it was feared it would be too late for many residents to tune in to the opening broadcasts. Local TV dealers said they were being inundated with requests and wouldn't be able to cope.

By the spring of the following year the 'growing web of unsightly aerials' was causing great concern and plans were drawn up to establish a Rediffusion service in Hemel Hempstead. A master aerial would supply pictures to homes via an underground cable. The system went ahead and served a large number of homes in the town for many years.

Hard to Survive

The new town of Hemel Hempstead had cost £21,500,000 by 1957. It was scheduled for completion in 1962 – the year in which the development corporation was scheduled to be wound up – by which time corporation chairman Henry Wells estimated it would have cost £36 million.

The industrial estate had attracted industries from all over the London area, but in November 1956 there were signs that many of those industries were not going to survive the new town's first 50 years.

Rolls Razor, which had been one of the first to move to Maylands Avenue in 1952, announced it was to close because of heavy losses. Rolls said they had sold their factory and land to Kodak and that was the first time that the name of Kodak became linked with the town.

It was, of course, the very first inkling of what was to become the colour processing plant where so many local people worked until it also became a victim of the march of progress.

Residents in Chaulden get into the swing of their fun day in the late 1960s.

The wind of change was blowing through Marlowes in 1954 – here you can see the new town market square taking shape.

Lockers Park School in Hemel Hempstead survived the new town revolution unscathed.

A trio of new schools in the early 1960s – Bennetts End, Hobbs Hill Wood and Chambersbury. Lord Silkin performed the opening ceremony at Apsley Grammar School – the man who, as a government minister back in 1947, had picked Hemel Hempstead as the site of a new town. Cavendish School began life in the Warners End Secondary School and its own new buildings were not officially opened until 1962 by Professor Nevill Mott, professor of experimental physics at the Cavendish Laboratory. In this picture, Professor Mott and Mayor of Hemel Hempstead Tony Graham watch a young scientist at work at Cavendish.

Kodak Colour Processing, the town's best-known firm, came to Maylands Avenue in 1956.

The factory of T. Foxall and Sons, a family business which moved to Maylands Avenue in 1956.

Although it was to be a couple of years on from 1956 before everything was up and running, the arrival of Kodak with its colour processing division on an 8½-acre site in Maylands Avenue was to have a big impact on the town from the late 1950s and through the 1960s in particular.

Marlowes in 1959 as the transformation gathered pace.

Miss Hemel Hempstead enjoys the spotlight in the 1960s.

Nicky Line Railway, as it became known, ran from the centre of Hemel Hempstead through Redbourn to Harpenden where passengers could link up with the main line through Luton to London. The main railway line we all know today which runs through Boxmoor and on to Berkhamsted, Tring and the Midlands, or to

Euston in the opposite direction, opened in 1837, but the station (in the same place as it is today) was called Boxmoor and was a long way from the town of Hemel Hempstead in an age when there were no cars or buses.

So lots of local people wanted a better train service and that – coupled with the need to transport the area's watercress – was how the Nicky Line came about. The line crossed Marlowes on a viaduct (bridge) round the back of what is now the Marlowes Shopping Centre to Hemel Hempstead Midland Station. That was opposite the Midland Hotel which still stands today in Midland Hill. The hotel was built to serve the railway in 1899.

The line ran across to what we know today as Highfield, but in those days was all farmland. In the Highfield area was a little station called Godwins Halt. This was named after a local man who owned land in the area. The line ran through Cupid Green where there were brickworks and on to Redbourn.

The railway continued to be used by both passengers and goods services right through until 1947. In 1947, the passenger service stopped, but goods traffic continued for many years. The line in the town centre disappeared as the new town was built in the 1950s and in 1959 the viaduct across Marlowes was demolished. For a time in the 1960s the line between Cupid Green and Harpenden was used by the Hemellite company based at Cupid Green, but eventually the whole line closed. It has now been turned into a special walk and many of the old bridges remain – the one across Queensway is probably the best known.

The Marlowe Viaduct has long gone, but many of the Nicky Line bridges remain.

Quiet, sedate and serene. A distant memory before the next chapter in Hemel Hempstead's history.

We Have Blast Off

THE coming of the canal and then the railway in the last century were the roots that led to the growth, not just of Hemel Hempstead, but of Dacorum. And of equal significance for the subsequent growth of the town and its surroundings was the opening of the M1 a century later in 1959.

The motorway's first fatality happened three months before the road even opened when a twin-engined plane carrying officials from the Tarmac company crashed while landing on the carriageway near Leverstock Green. Before the road opened it was quite common for planes carrying engineers to use the road as an airstrip.

The new road certainly opened up Hemel Hempstead's links with London and the Midlands for industry, but it also opened up the links for criminals. In January of 1960 came the first motorway police chase locally. Two men from Middlesex broke into a photographic shop in the town centre and stole goods worth more than £500. They were spotted by a police patrol near Maylands Avenue and pursued onto the motorway, where the police car proved too powerful and the chase lasted just 300 yards.

Major Changes

The 1960s began with some pretty major changes in the town centre. The new decade was only a month old when demolition work began on Alma Road (named after the Crimean War battle of River Alma in 1854) to make way for West Herts College.

Also disappearing was the Nicky Line Railway. Work began on removing the railway embankment in May 1960. This involved moving 76,000 cubic yards of earth and saw huge lorries using the bed of the line as a road to shift the earth.

The bridge itself came down in July. A crowd of several hundreds gathered to watch and it was not until the early hours of the morning that the action began using a two-ton weight suspended from a crane. It took 30 blows to bring the bridge down.

That very night local MP James Allason made a speech suggesting the bridge should have been left as 'the development corporation's triumphal arch!'

Work was getting under way on the creation of the Water Gardens, but in an editorial the *Gazette* questioned the wisdom of such a move. It pointed out that so much was needed in the town – playgrounds, meeting places etc – that £36,000 was 'too much to spend on the luxury of a Serpentine'.

Age of the Car

The age of the car had really begun and the development corporation was ready for it with the opening of the three-tiered car park on the junction of Hillfield Road and Marlowes.

The car park itself, built into the hillside, was described as 'unique and the first of its kind in the UK'.

It cost £40,000, but what really attracted the interest was the ceramic mural on the side designed by the famous cartoonist Rowland Emett. The mural had (and still has) Henry VIII as the central character on a white charger. There was a typical city gent with a bowler hat and umbrella gliding over Dunstable Downs and a typical Emett train to signal the local importance of the railway line to Euston. Queen Elizabeth II watched a Comet airliner flying over Hatfield (emphasising the importance of the aircraft industry in those days) and the scene also depicted Whipsnade Zoo, St Albans, Bovingdon Airport, George Bernard Shaw at Ayot St Lawrence and Berkhamsted Castle.

Cinema's Changing Era

The biggest excitement in the town centre was the opening of the new Odeon Cinema. The opening film was *Doctor In Love* and two of the stars – Leslie Phillips and Virginia Maskell – attended the official opening.

A seat in the stalls would cost you 2s 6d while the 'stadium seats' were 3s 6d. The opening programme included the latest from the *Look At Life* series and included footage shot in Hemel Hempstead.

The opening of the Odeon brought the end of an era – the closing of the Luxor in Marlowes. It actually closed a week before the Odeon opened, but the Princess, on the site of the planned new civic centre, carried on for a couple more years.

1960 also marked the start of the space age and the development corporation attempted to mark this by naming new streets in Highfield – Jupiter Drive, Saturn Way, Martian Avenue and Mercury Walk.

As the corporation's chairman Henry Wells put it: 'Highfield has been designed on somewhat novel lines and at the beginning of the space age – hence the names.'

If Highfield was entering the space age, Grovehill was just about ready for blast off in 1960. The revised master plan for Hemel Hempstead forecast the population of the new town rising to more than 80,000 by 1980 and a new neighbourhood called Grovehill was to be created on about 400 acres north of Redbourn Road. It would provide homes for 9,000 people.

'...Into a Homogeneous Whole'

By 1961 the borough's population had risen to 55,164 – very near the originally proposed 60,000 – but work was still going on apace.

Highfield was growing rapidly and in June the Highfield Neighbourhood Association was formed. Work had also started in Leverstock Green.

But one development not taking place was a new station for Hemel Hempstead. The British Railways Board announced that it had finally decided to reject the development corporation's original idea that there should be a new station at Two Waters.

However, British Rail did carry out a £60,000 scheme to revamp Boxmoor Station a year later.

There was much talk of another development – Dacorum Pavilion. The council debated the issue

of whether, if the town got government permission to go ahead with the £250,000 plan, it would be 'a white elephant or West Herts Mecca'. The council voted to go ahead and Alderman Gilbert Hitchcock said it would be an important step in 'welding the town into a homogeneous whole',

The body responsible for the creation of the new town – the Hemel Hempstead Development Corporation – was wound up in 1962 and replaced by the Commission for the New Towns.

Over 15 years the development corporation had transformed Hemel Hempstead and there was much interest in who would be appointed by the government to sit on the Hemel Hempstead committee of the CNT.

When the committee was named there was only one surprise choice, Mr Ray Harries who was the manager of Barclays Bank in the town. He had come to the town in 1948 and had been 'privileged to see much of this wonderful experiment taking place'.

A rapidly growing town needed a police force to match: neighbourhood beat bobbies reached Hemel Hempstead in 1962 and Hertfordshire's traffic police were launched in the same year. Bidding farewell to the area were the American servicemen based at Bovingdon, which had been a USAF base for 20 years.

Statue Crazy?

Is Hemel Hempstead going statue crazy? This was one of the big questions of 1962.

First, the development corporation commissioned French sculptor M. Hubert Yencesse to design a sculpture of two young people dancing for the Water Gardens. Next, development corporation chairman Henry Wells acquired two sculptures – one of two platypuses and the other of a kangaroo with a joey in its pouch – from Australia. They were installed below the Wimpy Bar in Marlowes, but the platypus moved to the Water Gardens when the Marlowes Shopping Centre was developed.

But it was the rash of sculptures that appeared in Highfield in August 1962 that prompted the

Gazette to ask if the town was going 'statue crazy'.

Some residents were not at all happy with works such as *Boy with Cat* at Hyperion Court and *Reclining Figure* near Martian Avenue. The Commission for the New Towns said the works encouraged Hertfordshire's sculptors and street art is something that has continued to thrive in the area – just take a stroll down today's pedestrianised Marlowes with its steel tree, rainbow, model town and fountain.

A Revolutionary Development

The town's new circular car park, the first of its kind to be built by Sir Robert McAlpine, was quickly taking shape in the town centre in 1963, but one member of the borough council thought more 'drastic change' was necessary. Alderman Wyndam Thomas proposed that pedestrianisation was the answer – an answer that was to come 30 years later.

One revolutionary development progressing well in 1963 was the Sheelmex BP office block across the entrance to Marlowes. It was groundbreaking, but one resident did not think the town had got a fair deal. He quizzed the district auditor as to why the council had not got £10,000 for the air the building would occupy across Marlowes! The district auditor responded that although the council owned the surface rights of the road, if it wanted to make a claim for the airspace above it would have to prove that the land itself had been 'vested in' the council.

Helping to ease traffic congestion around the town centre, Hemel Hempstead's new £336,000 bypass (Leighton Buzzard Road) was completed with the opening of the final section from Galley Hill to Piccotts End in July.

New Town Hall

Work was under way on the new town hall – Dacorum Pavilion – though it would be more than two years before the building was used. In April 1963 a time capsule was buried in the foundations. Its contents included a copy of the *Gazette*, the *Times* and a scroll of the names of the councillors. But as the new town hall began to go up the old town hall very nearly came down!

Councillors debated what should happen to the old building once they were installed in their plush new headquarters and old town hall came in for some withering comments.

It was described as 'a murky mausoleum', 'a graceless relic of Victorian pedantry', and 'an undistinguished and sad faced thing'. In fact, only the casting vote of the Mayor of Hemel Hempstead Tony Graham saved it from the bulldozer.

Maylands Avenue seen from the newly built Pelham Court in the 1960s.

The construction of the BP building– which has now disappeared – turned the southern end of Marlowes into a vast building site at the end of the 1960s.

The centre of Marlowes in the late 1960s.

The carnival rolls down Marlowes in 1967. You can see the BP building in the background.

And the carnival still rolls down Marlowes in 1967.

Hemel Hempstead's new sports centre would rise from the rubble on this spot.

Dignitaries burying a time capsule at the foundation laying of the new town hall.

In January 1956, Woolworth's moved from the High Street to its new premises in the heart of Marlowes.

The end of the 1960s brought another surge of activity in Marlowes. Work on a new Sainsbury's supermarket and Boots was under way.

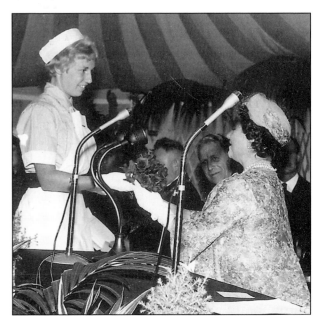

The Queen Mother's visit to the town in 1959 generated almost as much excitement as her daughter's visit. During her trip, she paid a visit to the home of the Burman family on the corner of Boxted Road and Peartree Road and also visited the nurses at West Herts Hospital.

More pictures of the Queen
Mother's visit to West Herts
Hospital, in 1959.

Lauren Bacall brought a little glamour to the town
in 1959 when she launched a new cinema on the
corner of Marlowes and Bridge Street.

Prime Minister Sir Alec Douglas-Home arrived in
Hemel Hempstead in 1964 to shore up support for
the embattled Tories before the General Election.
Their man – James Allason – hung on, but with a
much reduced majority.

In 1963, students moved from temporary buildings in Adeyfield to Hemel Hempstead's brand new college of further education in Marlowes. It had cost £346,000 and had 50 full-time students, 500 part-timers and 2,000 doing evening classes.

Youngsters turned out in force to greet the Duke of Edinburgh when he arrived at Bovingdon Airport in 1959 for a whistlestop tour to check on his newly introduced award scheme.

During the 1960s, new buildings were springing up everywhere. Workers topped out at the Pavilion (these two pages). Later the official opening was conducted by Roy Jenkins (page 96). The flagship project was being demolished as this book went to press.

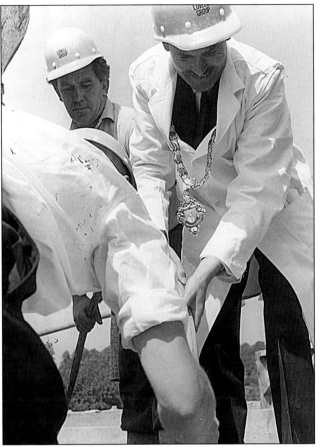

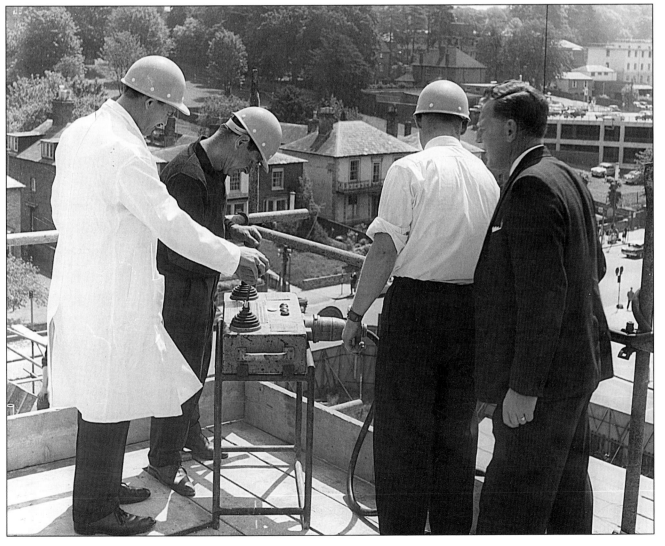

The official opening was conducted by Roy Jenkins, right.

The Luxor cinema was demolished in the 1960s. It stood next to today's Woolworths.

Two views of the Princess Cinema in Marlowes showing the projectionist's room with fire escape.

The opening of an Odeon cinema on Marlowes in 1960 generated lots of excitement, but sounded the death knell for the Luxor cinema, which closed a week before, and ultimately the Princess cinema, which struggled on for a couple of years. Eventually, the Odeon itself was replaced by the Full House pub after a period as a bingo hall.

Architect David Nye spared no expense when he built Berkhamsted's Rex Cinema. Nye's art deco design boasted an imposing foyer with twin flights of stairs leading up to the balcony, a huge chandelier cascading from a triple coved ceiling, art deco mirrors and an abundance of memorable plasterwork.

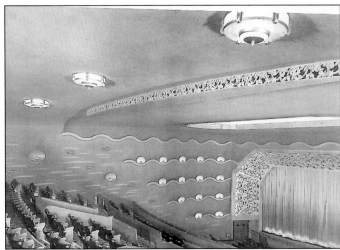

Left: The old police station on the Leighton Buzzard/Warners End roads was replaced in 1958.

The footbridge in Marlowes was supposed to help shoppers at a time when

the traffic still flowed down the street, but few people used it.

The Breakspear Motel – later to become the Post House – on its opening day in 1965. It cost £159,000 and had 28 rooms boasting black and white television.

The framework of Bank Court takes shape behind shops on the west side of Marlowes.

The new town had brought an end to many of Hemel Hempstead's old buildings, but no one was sad to see the town's Victorian workhouse at St Paul's go. Since the 1930s, it had been used as an old people's home by Herts County Council, but by 1966 a new home had been built in Highfield and the residents were moved out.

In 1967, it was announced that the old cottages in Half Moon Yard off the High Street were to be pulled down to make way for an £18,350 old people's day centre.

Hemel Hempstead's Old Town Hall was an established landmark by the late 19th century. In 1963, only the casting vote of Mayor of Hemel Hempstead Tony Graham saved the building from demolition. Only after that did it become a venue for the arts.

A Commuter's Paradise

THE overhead electric lines on the railway were switched on for testing in 1964 – signalling an end to steam and diesel.

It wasn't until the following summer that the electric trains made their debut. The new trains were set to make the line a 'commuter's paradise', said the optimistic report in the *Gazette*.

Commuters in their paradise had no 'page three' to ogle during their journey, but it was the swinging 60s and the subject of topless bathing arose at Hemel Hempstead's Churchill swimming pool.

The pool superintendent reported to the council that enquiries had been received about using topless bathing costumes and he wanted a ruling. The committee was told that the council's regulations already stipulated that if a complaint was made about persons at the pool causing offence, they could be asked to leave.

1965 brought news of two exciting developments which, if they had taken place, would have had a lasting effect on the town centre.

The Commission for the New Towns announced proposals for a luxury cinema, high class restaurant, hotel and car park on a site opposite the Waggon and Horses in Marlowes.

In the winter of that year came news of a plan for a £500,000 Army & Navy department store in Marlowes opposite Bridge Street (there was no Sainsburys or Boots in those days). Sadly, neither of these plans came to fruition.

But one town centre facility completed despite credit squeezes was the Water Gardens. It won a Civic Trust award for its 'charming and romantic transformation' of the River Gade.

Disappearing in 1966 were the bridges in Station Road which had once carried the Nicky Line trains laden with coal to the gas works.

The advances in industry and transport as well as oil-fired central heating meant a growing demand for oil and Hemel Hempstead, with its proximity to the M1, was chosen as an ideal spot for a storage depot. A two-day public inquiry took place into the plans for a depot at Buncefield where 150,000 tons of oil would be stored.

Full Steam Ahead

By 1967 it was full steam ahead on the last of Hemel Hempstead's new town neighbourhoods – Grovehill.

Other developments were to take place later, but Grovehill was the last in which the Commission for the New Towns was to have a hand.

The strategy for Grovehill, the first stage of which was known as Precinct A, was outlined to the world at a press conference in November 1966.

The *Gazette* summed it up thus: 'It has been called the very last word in housing. Its population may one day be able to own their own homes and it may be the answer to the new townies who seek a status symbol to match their increased bank balances created by making good in Hemel Hempstead.'

Grovehill was also different from the other new town neighbourhoods in that it was intended primarily for the people of Hemel Hempstead. The children of the first settlers were looking for their own homes and the growing belief in home ownership created its own demand in a town with so much public housing.

An idea used in the United States was behind Precinct A – the system used semi-prefabricated, semi-traditional methods of building and the idea of the maximum segregation of pedestrian and vehicular traffic.

A Controversial Plan

With Kodak and its colour processing plant in Maylands Avenue well established as one of the town's major employers by the late 1960s, the photographic company announced big developments in the town.

In March 1967 the *Gazette* revealed Kodak had been granted permission for a skyscraper on Aeroplane Meadow by the Plough roundabout. It would have 19 storeys and become the company's UK headquarters.

The news did not go down well with residents living in the Cotterells. Many felt the whole project had gone through the planning process suspiciously quickly and within a month there were signs of action on the site.

Although there was considerable controversy over the plan, it would ultimately bring jobs and prestige to the town and in 1968, as a goodwill gesture, the firm gave £10,000 for a new children's playground to be built in Gadebridge Park to replace the King George V playground which had been lost by the construction of the roundabout.

New Town Conservation

At long last, the old town got a boost in the late 1960s when it became the first new town conservation area in Britain.

Minister of Housing Anthony Greenwood came to open the conservation area in 1968 and a huge crowd gathered to hear him describe the High Street as the 'most beautiful in the county, and among the most beautiful in the country'.

With work on the last of the new town neighbourhoods well advanced, the first hint of Woodhall Farm surfaced in 1969.

The Brocks fireworks factory which occupied the site put in outline plans for a private housing estate of 1,500 homes plus schools. Brocks had had its factory on the land since the early 1930s and many people in the town worked for them.

Managing director Mr T.M. Bennett said the housing estate was a long-term plan and the firm would not move away overnight, but as it turned out it was to be early in the next decade that Brocks decamped and Woodhall Farm began to take shape.

Another major change sign on the horizon in 1969 was signalled by the headline: 'Bypass Route Settled This Year?'

The route of the A41 bypass wasn't settled – apart from the stretch around Tring – for another 20 years, but the wheels were already in motion.

In 1970, a report – *A New Town Comes of Age* – looking at the future needs of the community was published.

The population of the town as the 1970s began was already 69,500 – well over the original proposed final population for the new town of 60,000 – and later increased to 80,000.

The building of Grovehill was speeded up in 1970 because more new houses were needed to cater for the employment demands of prospering local firms.

The report proposed: new community centres for Leverstock Green, Grovehill, Apsley and Boxmoor; extensions to the community centres at Adeyfield, Bennetts End and Chaulden; a new youth centre on the site of the 16/21 youth club in Marlowes; Boxmoor Hall to be adapted as an arts centre for young people; the meals on wheels service to be extended.

Looking back now, just about all its recommendations were adopted.

Wiped Off the Map

1974 wiped Hemel Hempstead from the local government map: the reorganisation of boundaries that year saw the creation of Dacorum District – later to become Borough – Council.

Hemel Hempstead Borough and Rural District Councils as well as Berkhamsted and Tring Urban and District Councils were swallowed up by the new body.

But the reorganisation didn't impede progress – Grovehill was the last of the planned housing developments, but the completion of the new town did not, of course, mean the end of Hemel Hempstead's growth spurt.

Woodhall Farm began to develop in 1973 and it wasn't long before there was a need for still more development – Fields End became the controversial target.

With echoes of today's controversy over the need for new housing in Dacorum's Green Belt, Fields End was seen as the inviolable buffer between the town and Potten End.

But despite vehement protests, housing won the day.

Other developments followed, too, on the sites of new town schools which became the victims of what was known as 'falling rolls' during the 1980s – Bourne Valley, Highfield, Mountbatten and Halsey are all now the sites of housing.

Like the new town schools, many of the factories which had done so much to establish the new town disappeared as industry changed.

The Maylands Avenue of today with its high tech and company headquarters is unrecognisable from the Maylands Avenue of the early 1960s.

Similarly, the town centre of the early 21st century is a far cry from the new town centre of the 1970s.

The grand opening of Marlowes Shopping Centre in 1990 had a huge impact on the town.

The end of Hemel Hempstead Borough Council in 1974.

A youthful Terry Wogan visiting the bookies in Hemel Hempstead in 1975.

A fireman takes matters into his own hands during floods in the 1970s.

Kodak transformed Aeroplane Meadow with their distinctive headquarters.

The opening of Marks & Spencer in Marlowes was another decisive moment in its history. It was marked with a catwalk show featuring all the latest fashions.

And this was the Marks & Spencer fashion show for their opening at the Marlowes.

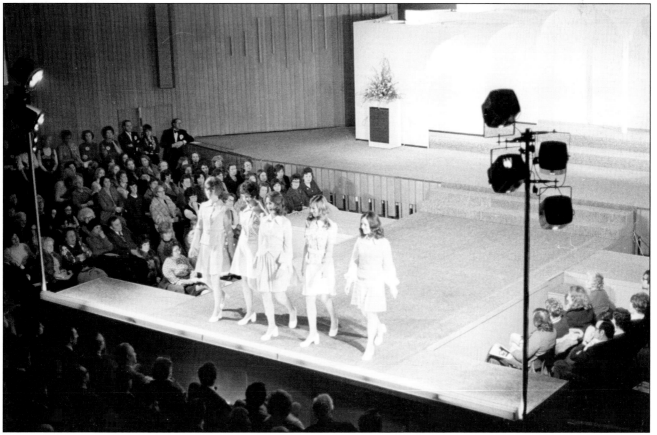

Hemel Hempstead's unique circular car park disappeared from the scene in the 1980s.

Power was in short supply in 1974 and many shoppers had to do their business by gaslight. For 3,000 workers, it meant short time and lower wages. Here, shoppers make the best of things in Snob Boutique, Hemel Hempstead.

The BP building that spanned Marlowes was revolutionary in the 1970s, but it became a victim of progress two decades later.

The opening ceremony of Grovehill – the last of the planned new town developments.

Along with Maylands Avenue, the history of Marlowes mirrors the history of the new town itself. Over the last 50 years, this pedestrianised area, which began life as little more than a muddy track in the 18th century, has become the town's commercial hub and experienced an unparalleled sequence of transformation that continues to this day.

Marlowes in the 1970s showing the site of what is today Marks and Spencer. It also shows the old BP building in the background.

Enoch Powell was a guest of honour at Norcott Hall in Berkhamsted in 1973. An audience of 100 Conservatives listened to him talk about de-nationalisation at a meeting of the Herts branch of the Monday Club.

Shirley Williams came to town in 1975 to open a new housing and community centre.

Look Motoring Supplies opened a brand new garage in Cotterells with the help of Screaming Lord Sutch and his fiancee, Thonn Rendesay, in 1974.

The opening of Marlowes Shopping Centre in 1990 was probably the single most important change in the turbulent history of the street. To make way for the centre, much of the 'old' town centre had to go – including the bowling alley and the footbridge.

By the time of the General Election in 1974, Hemel Hempstead had gone from being a safe Conservative seat to a key marginal. It was so important, in fact, that Labour leader Harold Wilson and Conservative leader Ted Heath visited on the very same day. Mr Wilson addressed a big audience at Dacorum Pavilion, while Mr Heath arrived for a televised 45-minute 'talk-in' at Heath Park.

In 1970, Earl Mountbatten returned to Hemel Hempstead, where he had once been a pupil at Lockers Park, to open a new secondary school named after him. Mountbatten

School has now closed and houses stand on the site.

The 1970 Hemex Exhibition at Dacorum Pavilion was the town's first industrial fair and attracted visitors from 11 nations. Many of the factories from Maylands Avenue took part and local industries paid a total of £40,000 for their stands. Here, the girls from Addressograph Multigraph demonstrate one of their magical machines.

Bob Bryant and Mick Workman were the first into Hemel Hempstead's outdoor pool when it opened in 1973, but despite attendances of 3,000 people, it closed the same year to make way for the construction of Hemel

Hempstead Sports Centre. The new indoor swimming pool – one of the finest in the country at the time – cost £1,300,000.

The borough of Hemel Hempstead was consigned to history in 1974 by the arrival of the Dacorum District. Dacorum's arrival also marked the end for Berkhamsted and Tring Urban and Berkhamsted, Tring and Hemel Hempstead Rural District Council. The town held a pageant and kings and queens of the past paraded through the streets.

This muddy building site eventually became Woodhall Farm. By 1974, Fairview Estates were constructing more than 100 homes amid the mud of the former Brocks Fireworks site off the Redbourn Road.

By 1976, work was under way on the new £29,000 bowls pavilion in Gadebridge Park.

Hopes that a new life had been found for Tring's former Regal Cinema, which had become an eyesore, received a setback in 1974 when councillors turned down a planning application to turn it into offices for *The Spectator* magazine.

Many of the new buildings from this picture of the town centre in the 1960s were demolished in the 1980s and 1990s to make way for new developments. Among the casualties were the BP building straddling Marlowes and Highfield School.

In 1967, the *Gazette* revealed that Kodak had been granted permission to build a skyscraper on Aeroplane Meadow by the Plough roundabout. It is amazing to think that this empty patch of land became the site of the town's most distinctive

Educating the New Town

THE provision of education and schools grew throughout Dacorum like it did in other parts of the country during the first half of the 20th century.

In Hemel Hempstead, by the time of the outbreak of World War Two, secondary school age children either wait to Hemel Hempstead Grammar School – if they passed the examination – or to Corner Hall Secondary Schools; there were separate ones for boys and girls. But the coming of the new town brought an explosion of new schools to cater for the vast influx of new families and the post-war baby boom.

In the early days of the new town there was a chronic shortage of school places.

It was estimated that all classes had 40 or more pupils, and children were bussed around the town to any school that could squeeze them in.

Between 1952 and 1970, schools just sprang up, but then came 'falling rolls' and many of those new schools closed or merged, and where they stood are now the site of yet more new homes. Of the secondary schools, Halsey, Mountbatten, Bonnie Valley have all gone. Apsley Grammar and Bennetts End Secondary Modern were combined into Longdean, and Highfield and Grovehill were merged into one.

The decline in pupils hit the new junior schools too, with one of the first to go being Maylands School which was itself the first of the new town schools.

The closure, and mergers were, in the main, fiercely opposed by parents but to no avail.

But those schools have not been forgotten, a fact clearly shown by the number of reunions organised by former pupils and staff.

Bourne End School, right on the edge of Hemel Hempstead. It opened in Victorian times and closed in 1937.

The scholars of Bourne End School pictured in 1929.

Bury Mill End School dated back to Victorian times but had been closed for some time when it was demolished in the 1970s.

Staff and dignitaries at the official opening of Corner Hall School in 1937. It had two separate 'departments' for girls and boys. During the evacuation of children from London early in World War Two, the premises were used as one of the area's dispersal stations and a double-shift system was required to teach the influx of evacuees from London. The buildings were eventually demolished and the pupils transferred to Mountbatten School.

The Building at Corner Hall School.

Belswains School was the first new school to be opened in Hemel Hempstead after World War Two, but it was not a new town school. It was a junior school and later an infants school was added across the school field. Today, the old junior school has been demolished and homes stand on the site, but it was rebuilt and survives on the site of the infants school.

Highfield School, another of the new town secondary schools that fell to the falling rolls of the last decade of the 20th century. It was combined with Grovehill School on the Grovehill site and renamed Astley Cooper. Again, the site of Highfield School is now new homes.

The staff of Bennetts End Secondary School in 1956, soon after it opened. Its sister school was Apsley Grammar. The two schools were eventually merged to form today's Longdean School.

Maylands School was the first new town school to be built and opened. It has since been demolished.

Bourne Valley School. It was one of the first new town schools to be closed and now is, again, the site of new homes.

These next three pictures show scenes from the official opening day of Halsey School. Established in 1961, the school moved to its permanent site in 1963 and did not officially open until March 1964. It is interesting to note that one of the governors of the time was one W.S. Cook, a man whose name would become synonymous with the naming of so much of the new town areas and roads. The school was named after the Halsey family of Great Gaddesden, lords of the manor and, at that time, residents of Gaddesden Place. Captain Sir Thomas Halsey was guest of honour at the opening ceremony. Now the buildings have been demolished and new houses built on the site.

Cavendish School in Hemel Hempstead began life in 1959. It was revolutionary for that time and was the town's first technical high school and as such regarded as the equivalent of a grammar school. But for its first two years it did not have its own buildings and shared with Warners End Secondary School (now JFK). Pupils were encouraged to stay on until they were 18 and the only difference between it and a traditional grammar school was that Latin was optional. The school started with 70 pupils who were selected from the 11-Plus examination. These pictures show the official opening day in June 1962 when, in its new home, it enjoyed a visit from Professor Nevill Mott, who was professor of experimental physics at the Cavendish Laboratory in Cambridge.

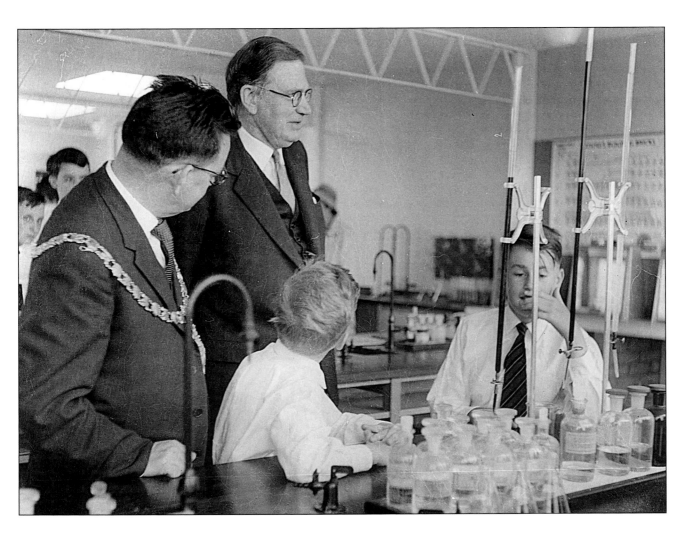

Around Dacorum

A CENTURY that brought dramatic changes to Hemel Hempstead brought change too to the other towns and villages that make up this part of Hertfordshire known as Dacorum.

Dacorum itself didn't get on the map until the local government changes of 1974. The end of the 20th century saw Hemel Hempstead lose John Dickinson and its paper mills, and for Berkhamsted too, the 1990s saw the end of an industry that since the mid-19th century had been one of its mainstays – Cooper's, animal health products.

Although it was to become part of Wellcome and later AgrEvo, to Berkhamsted it was always Cooper's with its buildings in the High Street, Ravens Lane and Berkhamsted Hill. Now, like Hemel Hempstead's mills, they have, or are becoming the sites of new homes.

But one large influence on the town and its prosperity, Berkhamsted School, remains strong. There has been change – Berkhamsted School (boys) and Berkhamsted School for Girls are now one, Berkhamsted Collegiate.

The A41 bypass should have taken much of the traffic away from the town centre in 1993, but a 19th-century time traveller standing outside the Town Hall today would still marvel at the number of horseless carriages, large and small, passing by.

The High Street itself would probably be recognisable, but change there has been. The Town Hall itself nearly fell victim to demolition, but is now again a focal point, although the seat of local government has moved across the road to the Civic Centre.

It was a century that saw the cinema come to and go from the High Street. First with the Court Theatre, opened during World War One and closed in 1960, and The Rex, opened in the 1930s, but for the last decade of the 20th century closed and vandalised to become an eyesore and the subject of much controversy. Today, as well as providing homes, the auditorium is being restored and soon the projectors are set to roll again.

Tring, too, has seen change. Despite the end of the Rothschild era, the influence remains in many buildings – Tring Park and the Walter Rothschild Museum. The High Street, like Berkhamsted, would still be recognisable to the 19th-century time traveller. The A41 bypass came much earlier to Tring and for several years was actually a fully-blown motorway – the A41M – before it was decided to scrap the motorway idea and get on with the bypass around Hemel Hempstead and Berkhamsted.

The silk mill has gone, but the name lives on as a road and district, and much housing development took place in the area to initially provide homes for people from the London area.

Berkhamstead High Street, west of King's Road, 1897. This building was once part of the Thomas Bourne charity school which was founded in 1737. It became the first home for Berkhampsted School for Girls before it moved to the present site in King's Road in the early years of the 20th century.

The High Street, Berkhamstead, around the 1890s. There is absolutely no traffic in sight, and three small children can stand in the roadway.

Northchurch, a village in its own right but thought of by many as a part of Berkhamsted. This is a view of the High Street in the early years of the 20th century but which today's motorists will still recognise.

The Cooper's headquarters in the 1950s, now the site of new homes.

The Court Theatre in Berkhamsted – where Tesco now stands – was built in 1916 to provide entertainment for the thousands of Inns of Court OTC men stationed in the town. For most of its 44-year existence, it served as both a theatre and cinema. It closed in 1960 and the supermarket giants moved in.

Views of Berkhamsted: the working canal in the 1940s (right) and the serenity of the town, including Castle Street.

Berkhamsted Station at the turn of the century.

Boxmoor Station – but the buildings shown here were demolished in the early 1960s.

Gadebridge Park before it passed into public hands.

Miswell Lane, Tring, in the late 19th century. Again there is no traffic to bother the owners of these fine houses.

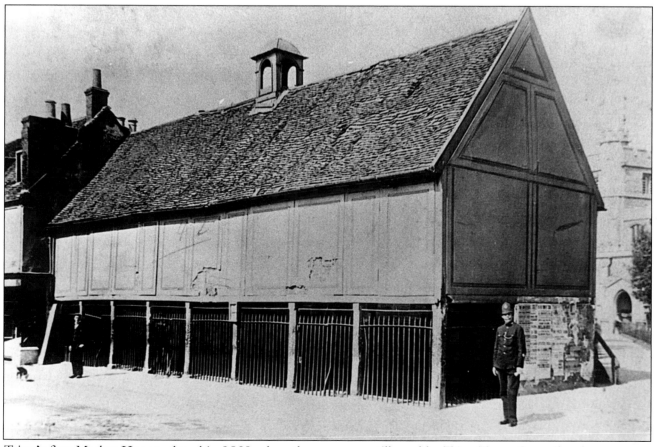

Tring's first Market House, closed in 1901 when the new one, still used by Tring Town Council today, was opened.

High Street, Tring, pictured from the Post Office, just before World War One.

Another view of High Street, Tring, this time around the turn of the last century.

Champneys, on the edge of Tring, is one of the county's top health resorts. Back in the 1930s it looked somewhat different with its 'chalets'.

The Tring of yesteryear.

The M25 is coming. Construction work on the Gade Valley viaduct by the Kings Langley section.

Opening day of the bypass – no traffic in Kings Langley.

It's a snip! The opening of the Hemel Hempstead and Kings Langley stretch of the A41 bypass.

Feet first – the opening of the Berkhamsted stretch of the bypass is just a few days away.

The first traffic begins to flow on the A41 bypass at Hemel Hempstead.

Not a car in sight with the new M1 two-laned motorway.

Above: Transport Minister Ernest Marples performing the opening ceremony at Junction 10.

The busy M1 over forty years ago.

What later became the A41, pictured in 1900. This is the scene in Apsley. No bypass was needed in those days.

Auguration Day, March 1958 for the Yorkshire-London Motorway.

The town's economic well-being has always had much to do with its transport links. It began in the 18th century with the construction of the Grand Union Canal, in the 19th century came the railway and in the 20th century the M1.

In 1959 Transport Minister Ernest Marples performed the opening ceremony at Junction 10 and made his historic 'calling all cars' message over a Herts patrol car radio to remove the barriers at all motorway junctions and allow vehicles on to the new road. Until the very last minute workmen with brooms were busy making sure the new carriageways glistened.

The M1 has come a long way since then. For a start, it's a lot longer. When it opened the motorway ran from Park Street, St Albans, to Dunchurch in Warwickshire – today the end of the M45. The Park Street to Hemel Hempstead stretch became the M10 when the M1 between Berrygrove (Bushey) and Hemel Hempstead opened the following month.

There were no crash barriers and no lights when the motorway opened and the section between Watford and Hemel Hempstead had only two lanes.

That early M1 – all 55 miles and 134 bridges of it – took just 19 months to build and involved a workforce of 700 rising to 5,000. The idea of a London to Yorkshire motorway was first put forward in 1945 by the Minister of Transport.

By the mid-1950s traffic congestion in Hertfordshire on the A5 (10,496 vehicles a day) and the A6 (6,887 vehicles a day) was becoming chaotic and a detailed M1 scheme was put forward in 1955.

Although taking much of the traffic off these A roads, the M1 was almost deserted by today's standards. In the early 1960s it carried 13,000 vehicles a day – this summer that figure will be nearer 200,000.

In 1959 the county's police force quickly became the acknowledged experts on motorway policing. When the M1 first opened Hemel Hempstead police station became the centre of excellence for motorway matters.

Until the coming of the motorway, police cars had been black – but it was soon realised that higher visibility would be needed on the motorway so each force was equipped with two white Ford Zephyr estates with flashing blue lights on the roof. The motorway police remained based at Hemel Hempstead until, in the 1960s, a new purpose-built HQ was constructed at North Watford police station.

Motorway driving was a whole new experience for the drivers of 1959 and the early 1960s. Drivers weren't used to long distances at high speeds and neither were the cars. Breakdowns were frequent and with no MoTs in those days police issued appeals for drivers with old or unreliable cars to stay off the M1. Sadly, accidents were soon to become a feature and hundreds of people have lost their lives on the M1 over the years.

The first ever 100-vehicle pile-up happened on the M1 in Herts in 1969 and multiple pile-ups, particularly on the two-lane stretch between Hemel Hempstead and Watford, became a feature of Sunday nights and foggy mornings in the late 1960s and early 1970s.

Eventually pressure led to the introduction of crash barriers. But the idea that the motorways are accident black spots is something of a myth. In 1960 the M1 and A1 – then not a motorway at all – both totalled 17 miles in Herts. A comparison showed that six people were killed and 92 injured on the M1, but 13 were killed and 261 injured on the A1.

Epilogue

THE development of Hemel Hempstead and its environs didn't grind to a halt in 1980. In fact, anyone who last visited Dacorum 20 years ago would struggle to recognise it now.

The transformation of Maylands Avenue and Marlowes, the town's principle arteries, has continued apace – and at the turn of the century, it shows no sign of slowing.

The beginning of the 1980s, in particular, marked the dawn of the second big wave of development for the town's centre and its newborn neighbourhoods.

The town's industrial area has expanded in every direction, too – an expansion driven by the high tech industries tempted to the area by Hemel Hempstead's enviable geography and transport links.

While Marlowes has flourished since the opening of its shopping centre in 1990, the diversification of shops and restaurants in the old town has partially rejuvenated the High Street, Hemel Hempstead's historic and still beating heart.

The legacy of Satellite Town No.3 has grown in every way – the outlying neighbourhoods have acquired their own characters, their own foibles; each has endured teething troubles – and made quantum leaps.

Yet the more or less constant residential development throughout Dacorum has still failed to keep pace with the demand for housing; a failure which has led to soaring property prices and their attendant social ills.

Perhaps this, in essence, is the greatest challenge facing the borough, and indeed the region, at the beginning of the 21st century: achieving the correct balance between protecting the Green Belt and providing a responsible level of new housing.

If the upheavals of the 20th century are anything to go by, Dacorum will find a way to overcome its difficulties – and continue to thrive.